T0345907

The Anchors in the Heavens

Other Books of Interest from St. Augustine's Press

The Anchors in the Heavens

The Metaphysical Infrastructure
of Human Life

Rémi Brague
Translated by Brian Lapsa

ST. AUGUSTINE'S PRESS
South Bend, Indiana

Manufactured in the United States of America.

1 2 3 4 5 6   25 24 23 22 21 20 19

Library of Congress Cataloging in Publication Data
Names: Brague, Rémi, 1947- author.
Lapsa, Brian, translator.
Title: The anchors in the heavens: the metaphysical infrastructure of human
life / Rémi Brague ; translated by Brian Lapsa.
Other titles: Infraestructura metafísica. English
Description: South Bend, Indiana: St. Augustine's Press, 2017.
"Originally published in French by Editions de Seuil, S.A., as Les ancres
dans le ciel: L'infrastructure metaphysique."
Includes bibliographical references.
Identifiers: LCCN 2017015748
ISBN 9781587310409 (hardback)
Subjects: LCSH: Metaphysics.
Philosophical anthropology.
Classification: LCC BD112 .B6713 2017
DDC 110--dc23
LC record available at https://lccn.loc.gov/2017015748

St. Augustine's Press
www.staugustine.net

Contents

Foreword

This book grew out of a series of lectures I delivered in Barcelona from March 23–27, 2009, while I held the Joan Maragall Chair there. I would like to thank the members of the committee for the great honor they did me by their kind invitation.

In accordance with the stipulations of the Chair, the text, which I prepared and delivered in French, first appeared in print in Catalan in a translation by Jordi Galí y Herrera.[1] My debt of gratitude to him, already substantial after his translations of two other works of mine (including a text unpublished in French), has thus only increased.[2]

In these lectures I present a number of ideas that I would also like to discuss elsewhere at greater length and from a somewhat different perspective.

The reader pressed for time may proceed directly to §8, at the beginning of Chapter III. The outline of the historical development of metaphysics that I attempt up to that point is too technical for the non-philosopher, and too cursory, absurdly so, for the philosopher. I include the outline only to provide something of a background for what follows it, and thus only with attention to what is most important for that subsequent discussion.

Laurence Devillairs and Camille Wolff made a number of very helpful comments on the texts. For that I thank them wholeheartedly.

Once again, Françoise, my wife, was kind enough to subject not one but two earlier versions of the manuscript to her critical eye. I owe her

1   *La infraestructura metafísica. Assaig sobre el fonament de la vida humana*, Barcelona, Cruïlla, 2010.
2   *Europa, la via romana*, Barcelona, Barcelonesa d'edicions, 1992, revised & expanded edition, 2002; *El passat per endavant*, Barcelona, Barcelonesa d'edicions, 2001.

for a great deal more than her editing, but it is much easier simply to thank her for that service.

Munich, May 2009, and Paris, October 2010.

For this second edition, I have benefited from the observations of my friends Thomas de Koninck (Québec) and Juan-Miguel Palacios (Madrid), as well as the comments of several people whom I only know virtually: Mr. Guillaume de Lacoste Lareymondie, who published a review of the present work on *nonfiction.fr*, and Mr. Pierre Larzillière, a Facebook friend. My sincerest thanks go to them all.

Paris, December 2012.

CHAPTER I
Metaphysics as Knowledge and Experience

You will have noticed that the subtitle of this volume contains the word "metaphysical", an adjective. Now this adjective is derived from the noun "metaphysics." And this noun, in turn, while today a single word, originally comes from a Greek phrase consisting of three: *meta ta physika*. But it is not immediately obvious why either of these two jumps—from the phrase to the noun, and from the noun to the adjective—should have occurred at all. In fact, they are no more self-explanatory than is the very meaning of that initial three-word phrase.[1]

1. From a Book to a Noun—and Then to an Adjective

To begin with, it is not obvious why a discipline—or a science, or at least a field of study in which certain kinds of questions tend to be investigated—called "metaphysics" should even exist. *Ta meta ta physika* was at first simply the title, and a rather problematic title at that, of a particular collection of Aristotle's lectures.

That title, moreover, certainly did not come from Aristotle himself. It appeared for the first time in the first century A.D. in a text by Nicholas of Damascus, which today we possess only in Syriac. There the expression was translated quite literally as "after nature" (*dᵊ – bātar kᵊyānāyātā*).[2] Was it a librarian who gave those lectures

---

1 See L. Brisson, "Un si long anonymat," in J.-M. Narbonne and L. Langlois (eds.), *La Métaphysique. Son histoire, sa critique, ses enjeux*, Paris/Québec, Vrin/Presses de l'université de Laval, 1999, p. 37–60.
2 See Nicholas of Damascus, *On the Philosophy of Aristotle*, books I–V, ed. H.J. Drossart Lulofs. Leiden, Brill, 1965, book II, p. 75.

}3{

the name we know them by today, simply classifying them by their position relative to other books on the shelf? Scholars had long believed this to be the case, but by now it seems doubtful. The most ancient catalogues of Aristotle's works, we know, do not list the texts on metaphysics immediately after those on physics, as one would expect on that hypothesis. Was it perhaps instead a way of describing their contents? If so, then the "after" or "beyond" (*meta*) could refer to the conception of metaphysics as a pursuit higher than physics; or it could reflect the intended temporal order of learning, in which the study of metaphysics was supposed to follow upon the study of physics. These two explanations, the "vertical" and the "horizontal" or chronological, are in fact entirely compatible. We might take one just as well as the other, or indeed both. For metaphysics deals with realities that we humans cannot immediately grasp: in order to do so, we have to rise above our everyday experiences. And this requires a formation which may take a very long time, and which must be undertaken in a very precise order.[3]

It was, at any rate, only with the translation of Aristotle's works into Latin, carried out for the first time in the twelfth century by James of Venice, that the original three-word phrase was condensed (since Latin has no definite article) into a single word, *metaphysica*.

2. A Philosophical Discipline

Metaphysics as a discipline thus takes its name from the title of a book. This derivative use of the term is first attested in Greek in an early third-century work by Alexander of Aphrodisias. There Alexander listed the "philosophical sciences" as "physics, ethics, and logic," to which he then added the somewhat awkward expression of "the 'beyond-the-physics' (*hē* [*sc. epistēmē*] *meta ta phusika*)."[4] In the ninth century, starting with

3   See, for example, Maimonides, *Guide for the Perplexed*, I, 33, ed. I. Joël. Jerusalem, Junovitch, 1929, p. 47; French translation by S. Munk, Paris, Maisonneuve & Larose, 1970 t. I, p. 114.

4   Alexander of Aphrodisias, *Commentary on the 'Topics'*, I, 2 (101a26), ed. M. Wallies. Berlin, Reimer, "Commentaria in Aristotelem Graeca [CAG]", II, 2, 1891, pp. 25–26, 28.

al-Farabi, the expression entered into Arabic.[5] It was likewise found in that language in the work of Avicenna—at least in the original, for Avicenna's medieval Latin translator did not preserve this sense in his rendering of the Arabic word.[6] As for what metaphysics was actually supposed to be about, Farabi cleared up a certain amount of confusion that had resulted from a tendency to tie metaphysics too closely to theology. Farabi instead gave it a distinct object of its own: it was the study of being as being, or being in and of itself, and its modes, or the states and conditions in which being can be found. And Avicenna pursued Farabi's insight by developing metaphysics as a substantial sub-discipline of its own among the other branches of philosophy.[7]

Inspired to a large extent by Avicenna, the fourteenth-century Franciscan John Duns Scotus attempted to establish metaphysics as a distinct and self-contained discipline in the Christian world. Like the other great Schoolmen, he saw himself as a theologian rather than as a philosopher. Metaphysics as such was thus not his principal focus; he addressed it more in order to give it an object—namely, being as being—that would clearly distinguish it from theology, his central concern, which of course had God as its object.[8]

In the sixteenth century, the Spanish Jesuit Francisco Suárez presented the great problems of metaphysics in a voluminous manual entitled *Disputationes metaphysicae* (1597).[9] His influence was

5   Al-Farabi, *Fî aghrâd mâ ba 'd at-tabî'a*, in *Rasâ'il al-Fârâbî*, ed. M.F. Al-Jabr. Damascus, Dâr al-Yanabia, 2008, p. 25.

6   Avicenna, *Shifâ'* (*Metaphysics*, I, 3), Arabic ed. G. C. Anawati. Cairo, M. al Bâbî al Halabî, 1960, t. XIII, p. 21, l. 12. I use the convenient trilingual edition (Arabic/Latin/Italian): Avicenna, *Metafisica*, eds. O. Lizzini and P. Porro. Milan, Bompiani, 2002. The passage to which I refer is found on p. 52.

7   See al-Farabi, *Fî aghrâd mâ ba 'd at-tabî'a*, op. cit. On Avicenna, see the little book by G. Verbeke, *Avicenna Grundleger einer neuen Metaphysik*. Rheinisch/Westfälische Akademie der Wissenschaften, Opladen, Westdeutscher Verlag, 1983.

8   See O. Boulnois, *Être et représentation. Une généalogie de la métaphysique moderne à l'époque de Duns Scot (XIIIe-XIVe)*. Paris, PUF, 1999, esp. pp. 457–504.

9   F. Suárez, *Disputationes Metaphysicae*. Hildesheim, Olms, 1965, 2 vol.

considerable, including—paradoxically, for a Jesuit—in the universities of Protestant Germany.

The metaphysics of the modern era emerged with Descartes's *Meditationes de prima philosophia* (1641). The "first philosophy" in the Latin title is a classic Aristotelian term.[10] But in the French translation by the Duke of Luynes the title became *Méditations métaphysiques*. The name of the discipline appeared next with Leibniz in his *Discourse on Metaphysics* (1686). Since then the word has been firmly fixed in place in the vocabulary of the Western intellectual world.

3. A Dimension of the Human Being

In this book I intend to highlight the connection between metaphysics as a discipline and the very humanity of the human being, i.e. what it means to be human. It may be that in some ways this connection is an obvious one, but we do not often thematize it quite simply because there is hardly any need to do so. It should go without saying that metaphysics is something that *humans* study and that horses, for example, do not. The same goes for the rest of philosophy in all the domains it comprises, and likewise for everything else that presupposes the possession of language: the natural sciences, art, law, religion, etc.

Yet there is an even more direct and more specific connection between metaphysics and our humanity, one that has attracted attention only rather recently. Far from treating metaphysics as merely one activity among others that we may or may not wish to pursue, Kant spoke of man's natural predisposition (*Naturanlage*) for metaphysics, the innate need that we have to address certain kinds of questions arising "from the nature of universal human reason" (*aus der Natur der allgemeinen Menschenvernunft*).[11]

Later, Schopenhauer, who to a large extent thought of himself as a disciple of Kant, went so far as to characterize man as the "metaphysical animal."[12] This is a very interesting expression. It appeals to the

10 Aristotle, *Metaphysics*. E, 1, 1026a16.
11 Kant, *Kritik der reinen Vernunft*. Introduction, VI, B21–22.
12 Schopenhauer, *Die Welt als Wille und Vorstellung*, t. II, II, Ch. XVII, *Sämtliche Werke*, ed. W. Löhneysen, Darmstadt. Wissenschaftliche

traditional definition of man as the "rational animal" (*zôon logon ekhon, animal rationale*), but in so doing it interprets that definition in a very precise way: the possession of the *logos* means nothing more and nothing less than the capacity to do metaphysics. That term first appeared in Volume II (which contains commentaries on Volume I) of Schopenhauer's magnum opus, *The World as Will and Representation*, in a chapter entitled "On Man's Need for Metaphysics." Already in the title we have another interesting expression. It suggests that metaphysics is an aspiration just as basic to us as the body's need for food or drink. Schopenhauer goes on to introduce the term in Latin, *animal metaphysicum*, and explains it by emphasizing the properly human capacity for astonishment or wonder (*Verwunderung*), which he says is heightened by our awareness that we all must one day die—two distinctive characteristics of humans that other animals do not possess.

The first idea, astonishment or wonder, has ancient and well-known roots in Plato and in Aristotle. Schopenhauer himself cites the famous passage where Plato speaks of the capacity to wonder (*thaumazein*) as being characteristic of the philosopher.[13] On the other hand, the element that Schopenhauer sees as reinforcing this capacity to wonder—namely, the awareness of our finitude and of the inevitability of death—was rarely taken as a starting point for philosophical inquiry in antiquity. For the ancients, death was instead the preferred metaphor for philosophical activity, as it appears in the *Phaedo*—as well as in what became the traditional definition of philosophy, a formulation drawn from that same dialogue: philosophy was seen as "preparation for death" (*meletē thanatou*).[14]

In 1903, Bergson published a long article entitled "An Introduction to Metaphysics." It represents an instance of the chronic tendency to try to situate metaphysics on the side of the thinking subject. Bergson defines metaphysics as the absolute possession of some "reality," a

Buchgesellschaft, 1980, p. 207; see also *Über die Religion, Paralipomena*, XV, §174, *ibid.*, t. V., p. 406

13 Plato, *Theaetetus*. 155d; Aristotle, *Metaphysics*. A, 2, 982b12.

14 Plato, *Phaedo*, 64a5–6 and 67e3. On its reception, see also the collection assembled by J. Salem, *Cinq variations sur la sagesse, le plaisir, et la mort*. Fougères, Encre marine, 1999, pp. 89–167.

possession brought about by an intuition that puts itself inside of that same reality. This is only possible, he writes, in the knowledge that we have of ourselves. Metaphysics is thus "an inner, absolute knowledge of the duration of the self, by the self." "This true empiricism," he concludes, "is the true metaphysics," which "can be defined as *integral experience.*"[15]

The existentialist movement (if indeed this is anything more than a label bundling together a great number of what in fact are works of very different kinds) made powerful use of the experimental or rather "experiential" aspect of metaphysics. This can even be seen in the literary forms that some of the existentialist authors adopted in order to express their thoughts. In 1927, for instance, Gabriel Marcel published a *Metaphysical Journal*. In his *Nausea* (1938), Jean-Paul Sartre—preparing, as it were, for his masterpiece, *Being and Nothingness* (1943)—used the form of autobiographical narrative to present his intuitions on the very nature of the world and on its irreducible contingence.

That was the mood in the air at the time, even among those who were not professional philosophers. Such was the case, for example, for the poet Antonin Artaud, who wrote, "In the state of degeneration that we have reached, it is through the skin that metaphysics will be made to enter (*rentrer*) our minds."[16] This is an interesting formulation in French. We might suppose that Artaud was using the verb *rentrer* (strictly speaking, to return or go back into) simply in the sense of *entrer* (to enter or go into), as it is often used in our rather unscrupulous parlance. If, on the other hand, we were to suppose that the word was actually being used in its strictest sense, then the statement would have to be understood as implying that something was being reintroduced after it had departed, or indeed after it had been expelled. Skin, the limit of the body, would then appear to be an unexpected but ultimately effective detour

---

15 H. Bergson, "Introduction à la métaphysique," *La Pensée et le Mouvant* (1934), *Œuvres,* ed. A. Robinet, Paris, PUF, 1959, pp. 1392–1432, citations from pp. 1402–1403, 1408, 1432. English translation by T.E. Hulme.

16 "Dans l'état de dégénerescence où nous sommes, c'est par la peau qu'on fera rentrer la métaphysique dans les esprits." A. Artaud, *Le Théâtre et son double.* Paris, Gallimard, 1964, p. 153.

permitting us to do justice once again to what the mind had perhaps wrongly abandoned.

A more general shift had to do with the rhetorical effect of the words: here, too, the term "metaphysical" took on a new color. Early in the modern era it had come to mean "empty, irrelevant, far from life." Descartes, for instance, describes the hyperbolic doubt that he practices in the first of the *Meditations*, and which cannot be applied to practical life (*usus vitae*), as "metaphysical."[17] For the radicals of the Enlightenment, simply hurling the term at an opponent in a debate would suffice to discredit him. Thus, to an objection posed by Jean le Rond d'Alembert in Diderot's dramatized dialogue between the two of them, the character Diderot scoffs: "Metaphysico-theological nonsense!"[18] In the twentieth century, on the other hand, it came to assume the heavier, more disturbing aspect of a kind of dread. In a text entitled "What is Metaphysics?" Heidegger, grappling with the question, answers that the fundamental mood or attunement (*Stimmung*) of metaphysics is that of anxiety (*Angst*).[19]

4. Filling the Void

The effort to bring metaphysics (back) into the concrete world is itself perhaps a way of compensating for something that has disappeared, as Artaud's line suggests (again, provided that we take it strictly). A number of thinkers in the nineteenth century had the impression that the existence of transcendent realities was no longer as obvious as it had been prior to their day (or at least it was no longer as obvious as it was often imagined to have been, in what may in fact just be a nostalgic illusion). We can find evidence of this from one end of Europe to the other, from the Italy of Leopardi to the Germany of Nietzsche. Even Auguste Comte spoke of "the growing fragility of the metaphysical foundations" (here

17   R. Descartes, *Obiectiones septimae ad Meditationes de prima philosophia*, *Œuvres*, eds. Adam et Tannery. Paris, Vrin, 1964, t. VII, p. 460.
18   D. Diderot, *Rêve de d'Alembert*, *Œuvres philosophiques*, ed. P. Vernière. Paris, Garnier, 1964, p. 277.
19   M. Heidegger, *Was ist Metaphysik? Wegmarken*. Frankfurt, Klostermann, 1967, pp. 1–19.

using the adjective in a sense other than the technical one that he gives it elsewhere).[20] But the same suspicion can also be found in authors who preferred to use terms other than "metaphysics" or "metaphysical." Thus Flaubert observed toward the middle of the century that "the theological base is missing."[21] It is interesting that both the philosopher Comte and the novelist Flaubert conceived of the metaphysical and the theological not as some sort of crowning moment, some lofty summit in the clouds, but instead saw it as something very concrete—namely, as a foundation. From this point of view, we might well borrow Marx's terms, if only to turn his schema upside down: the theological ends up being a "base," an "infrastructure" rather than a mere "superstructure" resting atop the economic order. It is in this sense that the subtitle of this book should be understood.

The sense of the loss of the theological grew even more acute with the "death of God." The theme appeared in those terms early enough— for example, in the young Hegel, in a line that could just be a reference to one of Luther's hymns—but it was of course Nietzsche who so splendidly dramatized the event in the memorable aphorism usually translated as "the Madman."[22]

---

20 "[...] la fragilité croissante des fondements métaphysiques [...]." A. Comte, *Cours de philosophie positive*, Lesson 60, ed. J.P. Enthoven. Paris, Hermann, 1975, t. II, p. 776.

21 "[...] la base théologique manque." G. Flaubert, Letter to Louise Colet of 4 September 1852, *Correspondance*, ed. J. Bruneau. Paris, Gallimard, "Bibliothèque de la Pléiade," t. II, 1980, p. 151.

22 G.W.H. Hegel, "Glauben und Wissen," *Werke in 20 Bänden*, t. II, *Jenaer Schriften 1801–1807*. Frankfurt, Suhrkamp, 1970, p. 432.

CHAPTER II
Putting Metaphysics Back in Its Place

The metaphysical void that the keener minds of the nineteenth century detected was the consequence of what has often been seen as the destruction and abolition of metaphysics as a scientific pursuit. The later emphasis placed on metaphysics as a lived experience was perhaps also a way of compensating for its demise as a discipline that had once been an integral part of the standard curriculum for the study of philosophy, right alongside logic, ethics, and so on.

5. The Modern Destruction of Metaphysics

Metaphysics has not enjoyed very good press in the modern era. Actually, it has sustained quite a few assaults. To keep things simple we might distinguish four, or perhaps even five, stages of a long-term campaign waged against metaphysics:

(1) First, Kant destroyed theoretical metaphysics by showing that it led to inconsistent arguments. This is the point of the "transcendental dialectic" of the *Critique of Pure Reason* (1781). Here Kant shows that pure reason, when left to itself in the speculative realm, where it is deprived of the safeguard of experience, can only ever end in paralogisms in psychology, antinomies in cosmology, and mere wishful thinking in theology. The Kantian critique does contain certain themes passed down from the tradition of the Greco-Roman skeptics, with its challenges to dogmatic (i.e. Stoic) metaphysics, or else borrowed from Hume's appropriation of these challenges. But Kant was not content simply to *note* the indeterminacy and the uselessness of metaphysics. He explained its failure by uncovering its causes, and in so doing he showed that its failure was necessary.

(2) Two generations after Kant, Auguste Comte brought the adjective "metaphysical" back into circulation. But now it had a pejorative connotation. Comte spent his intellectual career expounding the famous "law of three stages" through which, he argued, humanity had to pass. It was already present in his thought starting with his *Plan for the Scientific Operations Necessary for the Reorganization of Society*, composed in 1822 when he was only twenty-four years old.[1] Here he labels a particular phase in the necessary order of the mind's development as "metaphysical." It is, he writes, an unstable stage, and consequently a provisional one, situated as it is between two other phases: the theological and the positive. On this schema, the theological comes first and is rather more enduring; the positive is to come afterward and lasts forever. Comte further criticized metaphysics for being abstract and he treated it more harshly than he did theology, which in his view at least had the merit of affording a certain stability to the institutions of society and culture in the age that it had come to dominate.

Historically speaking, the Comtean metaphysical age corresponded roughly to the eighteenth century. This period was essentially critical toward the convictions of the theological age. Metaphysics, for Comte, was thus taken to be strictly negative, incapable of anything constructive. It was in the French Revolution that this purely destructive attitude reached its zenith.

(3) Nearly a century later, Rudolf Carnap and the members of the Vienna Circle, calling themselves "logical positivists," adopted a maxim from Comte's early period, but turned it toward a certain kind of scientism. The young Comte had formulated the following rule: "Any proposition that is not ultimately reducible to the simple enunciation of a fact, whether particular or general, cannot offer any real and intelligible meaning."[2] The

1   A. Comte, *Plan des travaux scientifiques nécessaires pour réorganiser la société*, *Philosophie des sciences*, ed. J. Grange. Paris, Gallimard, 1996, p. 272.

2   A. Comte, *Considérations philosophiques sur les sciences et les savants* (1825), *Écrits de jeunesse*, eds. P.E. de Berrôdo Carneiro and P. Arnaud, Paris/La Haye. Mouton, 1970, p. 326. This is taken up again in the *Discours sur l'esprit positif* (1844), 1, ed. P. Arbousse-Bastide, Paris, UGE, "10/18," 1963, p. 43, and then in the *Cours de philosophie positive*, Lesson 58, *op. cit.*, p. 647.

Viennese took this and generalized it. For them, metaphysics was made up of statements that eluded any experimental verification and which *were therefore* devoid of meaning. Carnap expounded this point of view in an article in which, in passing, he also offered a scathing critique of Heidegger's famous inaugural lecture.[3] Truth as Carnap saw it has no other place than in natural science, conceived on the model of classical physics. Consequently, in neo-positivistic rhetoric the word "metaphysics" became— along with "mysticism," "bad poetry," and various other endearing terms—one of the preferred terminological waste-bins into which non-scientific statements were to be discarded. And it was not just metaphysics: any normative statement that might concern morality or aesthetics was also to be rejected.[4] Metaphysics, for its part, could in no way describe reality, but could only express feelings about life.[5] Interestingly, however, Carnap did not deny the legitimacy of the need to express such feelings, and for this reason he counted it to Nietzsche's credit that he, at least, had only ever tried to express his metaphysics in a poetic style. In his own way, then, Carnap, too, shared in the tendency that I mentioned earlier that would shift the domain of metaphysics from theory to lived experience.[6]

We might note in passing that the genealogy of logical positivism, in spite of what its name suggests, is not entirely legitimate. For in fact Comte himself was in no way a partisan of scientism. Quite the opposite: he tried to subordinate science to morality, and even to limit the claims that science could make.[7] But a scientistic attitude came to dominate popular opinion, wherein it fomented a distrust of metaphysics. This scientism is hardly widespread among the best research scientists today. Yet it remains common both among the advocates of popular science and in public opinion.

3   R. Carnap, "Überwindung der Metaphysik durch logische Analyse der Sprache" (1932), *Scheinprobleme in der Philosophie und andere metaphysikkritische Schriften*, ed. T. Mormann. Hamburg, Meiner, 2004, pp. 81–109; on Heidegger, §5, p. 93.
4   *Ibid.*, §1, p. 81 and §7, p. 103.
5   *Ibid.*, §7, pp. 104–108.
6   See above, §3, pp. 6–9.
7   A. Comte, *Discours sur l'ensemble du positivisme*, ed. A. Petit. Paris, Flammarion, 2008, 5, p. 415; 1, p. 69.

(4) Heidegger used the expression "overcoming metaphysics" (*Überwindung der Metaphysik*) in a series of notes collected and published in 1954.[8] The oldest dates back to 1936, four years after Carnap's article. For Heidegger, this was not a question of simply leaving metaphysics behind us in order to move on to something else. Rather, seeing metaphysics as a movement that was bound up with the entire history of philosophy in its totality, he tried to show how when metaphysics had reached its completion it had ultimately taken the form of technology, and how it had thereby come to determine the very character of Western man in all aspects of his way of life. "Overcoming" metaphysics, or rather "getting over" it as one does a disease (*Verwindung*), would thus consist in returning to the forgotten foundation of metaphysics: Being. The idea here was to grasp afresh the relationship that Being maintains with the essence of man, in spite of centuries of misguided metaphysical accretions—a relationship that in Heidegger's view the traditional definition as "rational animal" could only partly capture.[9]

These four stages of the critique of metaphysics did not simply replace each other in chronological succession. The architects and advocates of each stage believed, whether rightly or wrongly, that they were each in turn taking up the results of the previous stage in order to push its conclusions even further.

6. Metaphysics as an Intensification of Physics

I mentioned that we might perhaps discern a fifth stage in the critique of metaphysics. This one is somewhat more difficult to grasp than the others, for it is less an explicitly argued philosophical thesis than it is a vague state of mind. But, within the context of the growing aversion to metaphysics, it corresponds to an interesting shift in the chief factors motivating this disaffection. What had long been disliked about

8   M. Heidegger, "Überwindung der Metaphysik" (1936–1946), *Vorträge und Aufsätze*. Pfullingen, Neske, 1954, t. I, pp. 63–91.

9   M. Heidegger, *Brief über den Humanismus* (1947), *Wegmarken, op. cit.*, p. 182; *Einleitung zu "Was ist Metaphysik?"* (1949), *ibid.*, p. 197.

metaphysics and what had been rejected in the three first waves of the critique was its prefix, the *meta-*. It was understood, though perhaps wrongly, as referring to a "world-beyond-the-world" or an "other-world," a *Hinterwelt*, in Nietzsche's play on words; and this was a world that was no longer wanted.[10] The imperative was then to take back the body's rights from the encroachment of the soul, those of the earth from the overreach of heaven, etc. This sort of rhetoric was first made famous by Feuerbach, and it proved deeply influential for much of nineteenth- and early twentieth-century literature. Consider, in France, Pierre Leroux; in the German-speaking countries, Gottfried Keller; in England, writers from George Eliot (herself a translator of Feuerbach) to D.H. Lawrence. All this took place as part of a revolt of the sensory against the Jansenistic, Pietistic, and Victorian brands of asceticism culturally prevalent at the time—or, more simply and more broadly, it was a revolt against the rationalization of life that accompanied the rise of the capitalist economy.

In the present day, however, it so happens that what people dislike about metaphysics is represented less by the prefix and more by the root, the *-physics*, which contains the idea of nature (*physis*). Metaphysics is felt to be an intensified version of physics. For a long time it was felt to be essentially what could be called a *supra*-physics, far enough "above" physics to have lost any connection with it; and in this sense the notion is even found in Kant, who uses the adjective "hyperphysical" and the noun "hyperphysics" (*hyperphysisch*, *Hyperphysik*).[11] Taken as such, metaphysics was reproached for having abandoned the natural world in order to indulge in endless flights of fancy. But since then metaphysics has come to appear rather as a kind of *super*-physics that would intensify all that is burdensome about the brute facts of nature—precisely by anchoring such burdens in a transcendence that would give nature a permanent foundation.

10 F. Nietzsche, *Also Sprach Zarathustra*, I, "Von den Hinterweltlern," in *KSA*, t. IV, pp. 36 and 38.
11 I. Kant, *Kritik der reinen Vernunft*, A773/B801 and *passim*, *Von einem neuerdings erhobenen vornehmen Ton in der Philosophie*, *Werke*, ed. W. Weischedel., Darmstadt, Wissenschaftliche Buchgesellschaft, 1983 (henceforth *WW*), t. III, p. 389n.

Our contemporaries regard with ever-growing impatience the constraints imposed on them by whatever is not chosen, whatever must simply be taken as given in life. Now the first of all these constraints is the natural dimension of our own being, namely the body (*Leib*). Consider, for instance, the pejorative usage of the term "biological" and indeed of "biologism" (in the sense of biological determinism).[12] The latter was devised as a rejoinder to be deployed against the adjective "natural" in debates on morality—for example, when "natural law" was invoked with a meaning other than that of the "laws of nature" discovered by science. This tactic actually masks the conflation of two very different concepts: on the one hand, nature as the Stoics understood it, i.e. as the order of things that man discovers through an investigation guided by reason; and on the other hand, nature in the Epicurean sense, i.e. as the raw, factual state of a thing, how a thing happens to be.

7. The Kantian Exodus

Let us return to where the critique of metaphysics ostensibly began—namely, with Kant. As with the genealogy that would trace the ancestry of logical positivism back to Comte, this line of descent must be examined carefully. Kant in no way intended to abolish all metaphysics. His critique aimed quite literally at "putting it back in its place" by driving it out of the theoretical and into the practical sphere, the realm of moral action. For Kant, this was reason's rightful domain. The Kantian revolution could thus be compared not so much to an emigration or a banishment, but rather to the end of an exile—to a homeward-bound exodus. In a letter to his half-brother, Karl Gock, the poet Hölderlin calls Kant the "Moses of our nation," i.e. of the German-speaking lands.[13] This reference to the prophet who freed Israel from foreign slavery and led it back to the threshold of the Promised Land is in fact a very fitting one—and its fittingness goes well beyond the metaphors that Hölderlin himself conjures up, which focus on Moses as a lawgiver.

---

12 See below, §22, p. 73.
13 F. Hölderlin, Letter to Karl Gock, 1 January 1799, *Sämtliche Werke*, ed. F. Beissner. Stuttgart, Kohlhammer, t. VI/1, 1954, p. 304.

According to Kant, metaphysics had to be reborn in the form of a "metaphysics of morals," which he saw as the only true metaphysics. To be sure, Kant always intended to establish a "metaphysics of nature" as a complement to the metaphysics of morals.[14] But during his own lifetime the project behind this somewhat strange, even contradictory expression never really made it off of the drawing board, and what Kant was actually able to accomplish was scarcely taken any further after the decline of German Idealism. Nonetheless, his project ought to be considered to some extent in light of our current concerns, for it is a particularly interesting example of the connection between anthropology and metaphysics.

Let us pause for a moment to gauge the scope of the revolution that Kant brought about. It will be worth our while, for the decision to topple metaphysics and cast it into the domain of morals was an immensely weighty one. With it, metaphysics passed from its traditional domain, which was, roughly speaking, cosmological in character (concerned as it was with the creation or eternity of the world, with the existence or non-existence of a divine Creator, etc.), and into the strictly human realm, where no one had ever before dreamed of situating it. This domain is the only one within which anything like morals can exist, for, as Aristotle had noted long before Kant's day, the gods are beyond virtue and vice.[15]

We might put it in different terms: metaphysics had previously dealt with things that one could only observe or contemplate (in Greek, *theôrein*)—in other words, with the theoretical. With Kant, it entered the field of the practical, dealing with action. And it is only man who can "act" in the strict sense of the term. Again, Aristotle,

---

14 I. Kant, *Kritik der reinen Vernunft* (1781), "Architektonik," A 846/B 874, with the strange formulation: "Die Metaphysik der körperlichen Natur *heißt Physik* [...]" ("The metaphysics of corporeal nature is called *physics*"); *Grundlegung zur Metaphysik der Sitten* [1785], Preface, *WW*, t. IV, p. 12; *Metaphysische Anfangsgründe der Naturwissenschaft* [1786], Preface, *WW*, t. V, pp. 13–14; *Metaphysik der Sitten* [1797], Introduction, II, *WW*, t. IV, p. 321; *Über die Fortschritte der Metaphysik* [1790], t. III, 3rd Abteilung, "Proto-Dogmatic Movement to the Supra-Sensible," p. 629.

15 Aristotle, *Nicomachean Ethics*, X, 8, 1178b8–18.

too, had similarly observed long before that animals do not "act" in this way.[16]

As a result we might say that metaphysics changed its underlying physics. It is no longer the *meta-* of the same physics. Prior to Kant, the physics with respect to which it had been the *meta-* had been above all a cosmology; it was ever afterward an anthropology. It was in this way that the question "What is man?" came to take center stage in philosophy.

From this shift we can understand the profound significance of the definition that we saw earlier characterizing man as a "metaphysical animal."[17] According to Kant, the cause of the insoluble problems that metaphysics kept encountering—before he subjected it to his critique, that is—was the simple fact that man lives in the physical world. His presence is not merely the terrestrial sojourn of some biped or other—just one animal, as it were, among many. It is the presence of *man as man*, defined as he is by reason, in the world of the perceptible. Carrying reason around with him as a fundamental characteristic of what he is, he thereby likewise gives it a presence in this sensible world. And on the level of man's own experience of himself, the presence of reason also represents a deep yearning that longs to be satisfied.

Within human rationality, Kant drew what is by now a well-known distinction between two faculties: the understanding (*Verstand*) and reason itself (*Vernunft*). Our understanding processes the given facts of our experience of the world. Indeed, it links them together precisely to make a world *out* of them. Reason, on the other hand, seeks unconditional principles; it is in essence metaphysical. This is why, even if the understanding is perfectly at ease in the world, reason, for its part, is not at home here. Just as we might do in a darkened house where we have never been before, reason blunders about everywhere, knocking into things and losing its way. The cause of the disease that the Kantian critique would treat is thus nothing other than man's *being-in-the-world*.

It might be entertaining to attempt a Gnostic reading of Kant. After all, reason here is not without its similarities to the soul in the way that

16 *Ibid.*, VI, 2, 1139a20.
17 See above, §3, pp. 6–9.

the Gnostics conceived of it, namely as something fallen into a world in which it is a stranger and from which it yearns to return to its origin. The fact is that it was only after Kant, and above all starting with Schopenhauer who claimed to be following him, that there emerged a philosophical and no longer a purely historiographical rehabilitation of the Gnostics from the first centuries of Christianity.

Kant himself, however, took his distance from the Gnostic temptation, albeit only in his third *Critique* (1791). There he argued that the beautiful is the "symbol of morality."[18] The fact that we are capable of experiencing a disinterested pleasure upon beholding what is beautiful, writes Kant, shows that there is at least some link between our *Verstand*-governed senses, by which we see that we are *in* the world, and our *Vernunft*-governed morality, which reveals to us that we are not *of* the world.

Perhaps we would be within our rights to go beyond what Kant had in mind by turning to the etymology of the word *symbolon*, from which our word "symbol" is obviously derived. In ancient Greece it meant an object broken into two pieces—a shard of pottery, for example—which would be shared by two families between whom there existed ancestral ties of hospitality. It would suffice to bring the shards together—in Greek, *sym-ballein*—to prove that the families belonged together, too. Understood in this sense we are *guests of the cosmos*. As long as we are in it, we are perhaps only standing in an antechamber—but we are at the very least welcome here.

18 Kant, *Kritik der Urteilskraft*, §59.

CHAPTER III
Nihilism, Pessimism,
and the Rejection of Metaphysics

In the tradition of the philosophers I have cited thus far, I would now like to say something myself about the relationship between metaphysics and the human being. But, quite obviously, I am going to enter the discussion on a level much more modest than theirs, a level much more flatly concrete. What I hope to do is to show how a certain doctrine that is central to metaphysics makes human existence possible, with existence here understood in the most banal sense imaginable: namely, the mere presence of our species here on earth.

8. The Rise of Nihilism

To that end, I will begin with a phenomenon of European culture that ran parallel to the abandonment of metaphysics, which it both intensified and radicalized, and which also had quite practical consequences: the rise of what is called nihilism.

It was at the end of the eighteenth century that the word first appeared, probably with Jacobi, who gave it a rather pejorative color from the start.[1] Thereafter, it pervaded the whole of the nineteenth century,

---

1   For the whole history of the word, see the synthetic account offered by F. Volpi, *Il nichilismo*. Bari, Laterza, 1996; on the beginnings of the story, see the anthology by Dieter Arendt (ed.), *Nihilismus: Die Anfänge, Von Jacobi bis Nietzsche*. Cologne, Hegner, 1970, introduction, pp. 9–106; on the basis, see S. Rosen, *Nihilism: A Philosophical Essay*. New Haven, Yale University Press, 1969; and C. Cunningham, *Genealogy of Nihilism: Philosophies of nothing and the difference of theology*. London/New York, Routledge, 2002.

first in Germany and then—and above all—in Russia, where it became closely associated with political terrorism.

Finally, nihilism came to be crucially important for Nietzsche, in whose philosophy it took on a quite specific meaning and played a very central role. Nietzsche believed it was destined to dominate human history for the next two centuries.[2] For him, nihilism was "the most disturbing guest," "the danger of dangers."[3]

Nietzsche's aim was not to resist nihilism by opposing it directly, as if trying to check its advance. He rather sought to overcome it precisely by pushing it to its logical conclusion. As he saw it, nihilism ought to be inverted so as to move from a passive phase to one of "active nihilism," in an expression that he probably used for the first time in the long fragment composed at Lenzer Heide (Grisons), dated June 10, 1887.[4] In its active form, he thought, and in the hands of the genuinely creative spirits among mankind, nihilism could become a truly formidable hammer of an idea.[5] But his instrument of destruction could also be turned to art: nihilism could, for example, eliminate degenerate and dying races, and in so doing could clear the way for a new order yet to come.[6] All this has a disagreeable ring to it nowadays. But to be clear, it was in no way a call for any organized famines, purges, or mass genocides of the kind that filled the twentieth century, not even for the horrific bombings carried out by Russian nihilists already in Nietzsche's day.

In fact, Nietzsche thought that nihilism had a much more immediate, immanent fulfillment, a peculiar deed or act (*Tat*) that is proper to its own nature: suicide. He lambasted Christianity, which he saw as a parenthetical interruption to the natural course of human history, for

2   F. Nietzsche, Fragment 11 (119), November 1887–March 1888, *KSA*, t. XIII, p. 56; see also (411), pp. 189–190.
3   F. Nietzsche, Fragments 2 (100), and (137), autumn 1885–autumn 1886, *KSA*, t. XII, p. 109 and p. 125.
4   F. Nietzsche, Fragment 5 (71), §13, summer 1886–autumn 1887, *KSA*, t. XII, p. 216.
5   F. Nietzsche, Fragment 2 (101), autumn 1885–autumn 1886, *KSA*, t. XII, p. 111.
6   F. Nietzsche, Fragment 35 (82), May–July 1885, *KSA*, t. XI, p. 547.

convincing people who really ought to have been "cleansed" that they were immortal, thereby making life tolerable for them.[7] In the normal conditions that he thought were to be re-established after the close of the long parenthesis, those who are unable to survive nihilism will simply eliminate themselves in a kind of natural selection. Nihilism, when pushed to its logical conclusion, would thereby overcome itself (achieve *Selbstüberwindung*).[8] Imagine, if you will, an arboreal parasite that thrives by living in and feeding on its host until it kills it—and then must itself inevitably die with the tree.

Along similar lines, nihilism assumed a sunnier mood toward the end of the twentieth century, notably in the work of the Italian philosopher Gianni Vattimo (b. 1937). His philosophical position is often called "cheerful nihilism." This expression is not Vattimo's, and comes rather from his elder, now-deceased compatriot Augusto del Noce, who used the term critically, as it happens, and with bitter irony. I do not know whether Vattimo himself has yet adopted it, but it conveys well enough his emphasis on what he believes are the positive aspects of nihilism, the opportunities that it holds for human freedom, and the possibilities that it opens for the peaceful organization of society. In practice, then, nihilism understood in this sense looks like the exact opposite of everything the term tended to evoke in Tsarist Russia: far from seeking to destroy, the cheerful nihilist is incapable of dying for any cause whatsoever, let alone of trying to kill for it, quite simply because there is *no* cause in which he believes.

There is a good chance that in certain respects nihilism is becoming very concrete, albeit perfectly unobtrusive. It is becoming, if not cheerful, at least *soft*.

9. Nihilism and Pessimism

Let us set aside for a moment the question of whether nihilism is something good or something bad. What does it actually mean? Nietzsche

---

7   F. Nietzsche, Fragment 14 (9), Spring 1888, *KSA*, t. XIII, p. 222.

8   F. Nietzsche, Fragment 9 (127), Autumn 1887, *KSA*, t. XII, p. 410; 13 (4), beginning 1888–Spring 1888, *KSA*, t. XIII, p. 215.

traced its genealogy back to pessimism.[9] For him, nihilism was first of all simply a clearer expression of pessimism, and could ultimately be substituted for it.[10] Pessimism as Nietzsche meant it should not be taken in the weaker sense that it has today, namely, a basically psychological one. It should instead be understood first of all in the strict sense given it by Schopenhauer, who may also have coined the term. Schopenhauer himself was trying to take a stance diametrically opposed to optimism. Now optimism, for its part, was probably not the invention of any philosopher. It was very likely Voltaire who coined it in his *Candide* (1759), where he mocks the worldview expounded in Leibniz's *Théodicée* (1710). Optimism posits that this present world is the best of all possible worlds, that a world better than this one is simply impossible. For a better world to exist, certain mutually exclusive conditions, or states of reality that are not "compossible" with each other, would have to be realized simultaneously, and of course this cannot be. Conversely, pessimism in the strict sense posits that the world that exists is the *worst* of all worlds, and that it simply could not exist if it were any worse than it already is. Let us note in passing that the idea that a *totally* bad world, a sort of hell, simply could not exist is itself a final tribute paid to the old identity of Being and the Good—a theme to which I shall soon return—just as hypocrisy is homage rendered to virtue by vice.

Nietzsche, for his part, then proposed a modified definition of nihilism. It is the process by which the highest values devalue themselves, and it proceeds, he said, from a radical rejection of value, of meaning, and everything that might make something desirable.[11] Ultimately, it finds its most complete form in the conviction that existence itself is untenable, joined to the intuition that we have no right to claim the existence of any kind of realm beyond appearances that could redeem the things that we do see before us.[12]

---

9   F. Nietzsche, Fragment 35 (45), May–July 1885, *KSA*, t. XI, p. 532; 2 (131), Autumn 1885–Autumn 1886, *KSA*, t. XII, p. 129; 9 (107), autumn 1887, *ibid.*, p. 396; 10 (192), *ibid.*, p. 571.
10 F. Nietzsche, Fragment 17 (3), May–June 1888, §3, *KSA*, t. XIII, p. 522.
11 F. Nietzsche, Fragment 2 (127), Autumn 1885–Autumn 1886, *KSA*, t. XII, p. 125, and Fragment 9 (35), Autumn 1887, *ibid.*, p. 350.
12 F. Nietzsche, Fragment 10 (192), Autumn 1887, *KSA*, t. XII, p. 571.

To understand this definition, we of course must first understand what is meant by "values." But the use of that term values is itself the result of a transformation of the way in which "good" was understood. It is a term that ought to be examined like a symptom in a medical case and not taken as self-evident.

At the moment, though, I would propose that we step back in order to approach nihilism by a way that is itself negative, starting with the word's etymology. It is obviously derived from the Latin *nihil*, "nothing." I would thus begin by asking *what sort of being* it is whose nothingness, so to speak, nihilism is so interested in affirming. Now it seems clear to me that nihilism, as we saw Nietzsche himself define it just now, amounts to an attack on a very particular claim of classical metaphysics, and a claim very central to it at that. It runs from one end to the other of the classical tradition, and was ultimately the basis for Leibniz's "optimism."

The claim I have in mind is what the Scholastics traditionally called the "convertibility of the transcendentals." This is a technical term meaning the following: that all that is, insofar as it *is*, is also *one*, *good*, and *true*. The part of this teaching that is especially pertinent in the present context is the identification of Being and Goodness.[13] It governs the relationship between what *is* and what *ought to be*, conceiving of this identity as being so profound that being itself has value, has worth; or, put differently, that being is "worth it," that it is "worth it" to be.

In what follows, then, rather than speaking of metaphysics more generally, I will focus almost exclusively on the quite fundamental claim that being is good.

10. The Convertibility of the Transcendentals

The convertibility of the transcendentals can already be found in the writings of certain Greek philosophers, where it is asserted two or three times, more or less explicitly, in the form of a very simple equation: that which *is*, is good.

Aristotle for his part affirmed as much within the framework of his overarching view of nature, which as he judged it always strives to attain

---

13   See J. Van de Wiele, "Het thema 'ens et bonum convertuntur,'" in *Tijd-schrift voor Filosofie*, 26 (1964): pp. 186–252.

what is best.[14] Now, for the good man, the "serious" man (*ho spoudaios*), being is a good.[15] But that is because this sort of man perceives reality not from a subjective point of view, but just as it is, without the distortions that warp the wicked man's point of view. And so since being is good, the things that are, by the very fact that they are, are good. The same claim can be found in the work of Aristotle's immediate successor at the Lyceum, Theophrastus: "The things that are, are in fact good" (*ta* [...] *onta kalōs etukhen onta*).[16] And it is found again in the form of a comparative statement that Aristotle himself had already made on at least one earlier occasion: "Being is better than Non-being" (*beltion ... to einai tou mē einai*).[17]

Later, some thinkers would be more radical and would state the equation in its positive form quite explicitly: Being is identical to the Good. Plotinus put it thus: "Being is desirable, because it is *identical to the Beautiful*, and the Beautiful is lovable, because Being itself is lovable" (*dio kai to einai potheinon estin, hoti tauton hō kalō, kai to kalon erasmion, hoti to einai*).[18] This Neo-Platonic thesis found its way into the Arab and persisted through the Latin Middle Ages, in particular by way of the *Liber de causis*.[19]

---

14 Aristotle, *Physics*. VIII, 6, 259a10–12; *On the Heavens*, II, 5, 288a2–3; *On Sleep*, 2, 455b17–18; *Parts of Animals*, I, 5, 645a16–26; *Generation of Animals*, I, 4, 717a15–16, and II, 6, 744b16–20.

15 Aristotle, *Eudemian Ethics*. I, 8, 1217b25–35; *Nicomachean Ethics*, IX, 4, 1166a19.

16 Theophrastus, *Metaphysics*, eds. A. Laks and G. Most. Paris, Les Belles Lettres, 1993, IX, §32, 11a26, p. 21.

17 Aristotle, *Generation of Animals*, II, 1, 731b30.

18 Plotinus, *Enneads*, V, 8 (31), 9, 40–41 (emphasis mine). See also V, 5, (32), 9, 37–38 (implicitly). These two passages have no equivalent in the Arabic *Theology of Aristotle*.

19 *Liber de causis*, XIX (XX), §158, Arabic ed. O. Bardenhewer. Freiburg im Breisgau, Herder, 1882, p. 96: *Wa-l-khayr wa-l-huwiyya shay'wâhid*; Latin ed. A. Schönfeld. Hamburg, Meiner, 2003, p. 43: *bonitas (et virtus) et ens sunt res una*. The passage has no clear equivalent in the corresponding passage from Proclus, who elsewhere even maintains the contrary. See Proclus, *Elements of Theology*, §8, ed. E.R. Dodds. Oxford, Clarendon Press, 1933, pp. 8, 32–10, 2.

For Aristotle, there were two reasons for identifying Being with the Good. First, Being is determinate (*hōrismenon*).[20] Aristotle here stands in continuity with his teacher, Plato, who had insisted on the link between goodness on the one hand, and measure and proportion on the other.[21] Second, Being is the object of universal desire: all things desire Being.[22]

What the Greeks of the classical philosophical tradition affirmed can also be found in the other source of occidental culture, namely the Bible. On this question the two symbolic cities of Athens and Jerusalem are in agreement. The very same assertion about Being is implicit in the first account of the act of Creation, when the Creator expresses his admiration for what he has made.[23] God's works are already "good" when taken day by day, piece by piece. Once beheld in all its perfection, the totality of Creation is "very good"—in a Hebrew phrase that also means "very beautiful" (*tov meod*, Genesis 1:31). Schopenhauer seems to have been irritated to no end by this passage and cites it directly in the Septuagint Greek (*panta kala lian*) on several occasions.[24] He detested the Old Testament and indeed everything Jewish, but he was at least lucid enough to identify his enemies here quite precisely.

In later Judaism, the sages of the Talmud commented on the Bible's rather strong claim about the goodness of being, and sometimes modified or added to it. One of them, employing an interpretive maneuver common at the time, even suggested that the passage should be read as *tov mawet*, i.e. "death is a good," thereby turning the original affirmation of being into what seems to be the most irreconcilable rejection of it that one could imagine.[25]

---

20 Aristotle, *Nicomachean Ethics*, IX, 9, 1170a19–21.
21 Plato, *Philebus*, 25de and 64d–66e.
22 Aristotle, *Nicomachean Ethics*, IX, 9, 1170a26–27.
23 It is amusing to note that L. Shestov, in his own *Athens and Jerusalem*, emphasizes Plotinus' echo of *Genesis*: see *Atene e Gerusalemme*, I, 7, ed. A. Paris. Milan, Bompiani, 2005, p. 304.
24 A. Schopenhauer, *Die Welt als Wille und Vorstellung*, II, 4, Ch. XLVIII, *op. cit.*, t. II, p. 795 and *passim*.
25 Rabbi Meir in *Bereshit Rabba*, 9, 5, eds. J. Theodor and H. Albeck. Jerusalem, Wahrmann, 1965, t. I, p. 70. Meir's exegesis is cited again in the eleventh century by Rachi *ad loc.*, in *Miqra'ôt gedôlôt*. Jerusalem, Eshkol, 1976, p. 8b.

The Middle Ages witnessed the confluence of these Greek and Jewish currents of thought. It is no surprise that the identification of Being and the Good should have been discussed by thinkers belonging to the three religions in the cultural contexts of which philosophy was continuing to develop at the time. Among Muslims, we might cite Avicenna as an example: "That which is truly the object of desire is Being; consequently, being is Pure Good and Pure Perfection" (*fa-yakûna al-mutashawwaq bi-l-haqîqah al-wujûd, fa-l-wujûd khayr mahd wa-kamâl mahd*).[26] Among Jews, we run into essentially the same statement in Maimonides: "[A]ll Being is good; everything is good because it is Being" (*wa-kullu wujûd khayr* [...] *kulluhu khayran idh huwa wujûd*).[27]

In the Latin West, the identification of Being and the Good was even formalized in the doctrine of the transcendentals, to which I have already alluded. As I noted, the transcendentals were called "convertible," which is to say that in anything of which any one of the transcendentals can be predicated, all the rest are also true: being, one, good, true—all these coincide.

More particularly, this teaching maintains that all that is, by the simple fact that it is, is good. This identification is already in Augustine: "All [...] that is, insofar as it is, is good" (*omne* [...] *quod est, in quantum est, est bonum*).[28] Thomas Aquinas took up this affirmation and treated it systematically, devoting an article of the *Summa theologica* to the question.[29] There again, all that is, insofar as it is, is good. As Thomas explains it, whatever is, is in act, and every act is a completion or perfection. But every perfection is the object of desire, and the Good is

---

26   Avicenna, *Shifâ'* (*Metaphysics*), VIII, 6, Arabic ed., *op. cit.*, p. 355, 14–16/806; Latin ed., *Liber de philosophia prima sive scientia divina*, ed. S. van Riet. Leuven/Leiden, Peeters/Brill, 1980, p. 412: *Id ... quod vere desideratur est esse, et ideo* esse est bonitas pura et perfectio pura.

27   Maimonides, *Guide for the Perplexed*, III, 10, 5–6, ed. I. Joël, *op. cit.*, p. 317; French translation *op. cit.*, pp. 63–64.

28   Augustine, *De diversis quaestionibus LXXXIII*, §24, ed. A. Mutzenbecher (CCSL, XLIVA). Turnhout, Brepols, 1975, p. 29; see also *De vera religione*, 11, 21 (BA, VIII). Paris, Desclée De Brouwer, 1951, p. 52.

29   Thomas Aquinas, *Summa theologica*, Ia, q. 5, a. 3: *Utrum omne ens sit bonum.* See also *De veritate*, q. 21, a. 2.

precisely what all things truly desire when they desire anything at all. Elsewhere he is more explicit: "All [...] that is, insofar as it is, is necessarily good; for indeed, each particular thing loves its being and desires to preserve it; and the indication of this is that every being strives against its own corruption" (*Omne* [...] *enim quod est, inquantum est ens, necesse est esse bonum: esse namque suum unumquodque amat et conservari appetit; signum autem est, quod contra pugnat unumquodque suae corruptioni*).[30]

11. The Desire for the Good

The telltale sign of the identity between Being and the Good, on this account, is thus the *desire to be* that we encounter in all things, as Aristotle, Avicenna, and Thomas Aquinas all observed. So our inquiry depends on the value that this desire ought to be accorded.

Classical metaphysics took the universal desire or end-oriented striving of things as a kind of prefiguration or primitive version of the human faculty of the will. According to the Stoic definition, the will is precisely desire illuminated by reason.[31] In irrational beings, on the other hand, desire is guided by something else instead of reason: in animals, by instinct; in plants, by faculties that are still more mute and obscure—all the more so in the case of minerals.

The Good, as the object of the will or of its more primitive prefigurations in irrational beings, can vary from case to case. The good that a rock "wants" in tumbling toward its natural place as it falls is not the same kind of thing as the good that a plant "wants" when it spreads its shoots aboveground and pushes its roots deeper into the soil below. Nor

---

30 Thomas Aquinas, *Summa contra gentiles*, II, 41. Rome, Editio leonina manualis, 1934, p. 131b; his *De veritate* cites Boethius, *Consolation of Philosophy*, III, prose 11, ed. H.F. Steward *et al.*, Cambridge (Mass.), Heinemann/Loeb, 1973, p. 288. See also Meister Eckhart, *Liber parabolarum genesis*, n. 103, *Lateinische Werke*, ed. K. Weiss. Stuttgart, Kohlhammer, 1964, t. I, pp. 568–569.

31 Cicero, *Tusculanes*, IV, 6, 12. Paris, Les Belles Lettres, 1968, t. II, p. 60. For the context, see *Stoicorum veterum fragmenta*, ed. H. von Arnim. Stuttgart, Teubner, 1978, t. III, §§431–442, pp. 105–108.

is it the same good that an animal "wants" when it goes about its quests for food and sexual partnership. Finally, it coincides even less with the good that man *wants*—this time in the proper sense of the term—in any instance across the whole spectrum of his activities.

Thomas Aquinas framed this relationship to the Good within a more or less explicit theory of Divine Providence. At its center is the claim that Providence finds its concrete expression in a graduated way all along the whole scale of being.[32] At the very bottom of the ladder, the good is simply the tendency toward self-preservation, as in the continuity of minerals or in that of a species as a whole. But the higher one climbs—up through plants, animals, and humans—the freer a thing's tendency toward the Good becomes in terms of its choice of means for attaining the end that it seeks. The tendency likewise becomes an increasingly conscious one, and one illuminated by reason; finally, the Good becomes less and less bound to coincide with the self of the desiring subject. "Good" ultimately no longer means merely "good for me." With this, the subject rises to a new level, the level of freely submitting to the very law by which the good for all things is established. In its highest expression, the act of the will may culminate in self-sacrifice, which is to say in the renunciation of self-preservation for the sake of a beloved being or beings.

---

32 Thomas Aquinas, *Summa contra gentiles*, III, 111 *sq.*

CHAPTER IV
Being as Mere Existence,
Life as Mere Contingency

We have seen that nihilism is a "no" opposed to a "yes." But I described this yes rather hastily. The yes that nihilism flatly rejects is the positive metaphysical claim of the identity of Being and Goodness. This claim, though, obviously presupposes some understanding of what "being" actually means. And it can mean quite a few different things.

12. The Reduction of Being to Existence

The notion of Being has traced a long and winding route through the history of Western thought. There is no way I can outline it in this book in even the most cursory fashion. I shall be content in this context simply to take a look at a particular turn in the history of the notion that I believe has proved decisive for, among other things, our self-understanding as human beings. It is the part of the story in which being found itself reduced in meaning to mere existence, while existence was reduced to pure contingency.

The first step was probably taken at the very moment that metaphysics was established as a discipline, i.e. in the work of Avicenna. His system rests upon a key metaphysical claim that is made clearest in a text likely written by one of his associates: being (*wujûd*) is something that "happens" or "occurs" (*'ârid*) to *a* being, i.e. to anything that is.[1]

1   Pseudo-Farabi, *The Gems of Wisdom*, ed. M.H. al-Yâsîn. Qom, Bidar, 1405h., p. 48; see A.-M. Goichon, *La Distinction de l'essence et de l'existence d'après Ibn Sina (Avicenne)*. Paris, Desclée de Brouwer, 1937, p. 133.

But this does not mean that being is within things as an accident (*'arad*) as Averroes would later misinterpret the line, perhaps deliberately.[2] Rather, it is a state that, when it "comes to" or even "befalls" the essence of a thing, does so, as it were, from without—the Latin is *contingere*. Being is thus in a way "contingent." When existence occurs to an essence, i.e. when an essence happens to exist in the world, this fact does not add any further determination—and certainly no value-laden determination—to the content of that essence. All it does is give it a place within the whole of being, as a particular thing. If it is good, then this is because the whole of being is still, in Avicenna's schema, tied to goodness: but the fact of existing, i.e. being something particular in the world, adds no goodness at all. In other words, essence is indifferent with respect to what just prior to Kant's time would be called the categories of modality. For Avicenna, there is no more "horseness" in a horse that really exists in the world, for example, than there is in the same horse considered as being merely possible; nor is there any more "horseness" in a necessary horse than in one that simply happens to exist.

Now, afterward, the whole range of *being*'s meanings was to be reduced to merely that of *existence*. As a result, existence, taken in Avicenna's strictly factual sense ("it is the case that there is a horse") and no longer thought to have any inherent value or worth, was neutralized, cut off entirely from the light of the good.

In this connection we ought to note how what we now know as values, for their part, arrived on the philosophical scene as if to compensate for the disappearance of the intrinsic good from beings, from things themselves. Values are a means of conferring on things—from outside of them—whatever sense of goodness seemingly ought to remain after their intrinsic goodness has been drained away. They were first explicitly named and discussed in the nineteenth century, initially by Hermann

---

2   Averroès, *Talkhîs mâ ba'd al-tabî'a (Épitomé de la Métaphysique)*, I, 6, ed. U. Amîn. Cairo, M. al-Bâbî al-Halabî, 1958, pp. 10–11. See also *Incohérence de l'incohérence*, V, §31–33, ed. M. Bouyges. Beirut, Dar el-Machreq, 1987, 2ⁿᵈ ed., pp. 303–305: existence is said to be added (*zâ'id*) to the essence of a thing. Lastly, see *Grand Commentaire à la Métaphysique*, Γ, C 3, e–f, ed. M. Bouyges. Beyrouth, Dar el-Machreq, 1967, 2ⁿᵈ ed., pp. 313–314 (concerning the One).

Lotze, who today is a rather forgotten figure, and later by Nietzsche. From then on, values were themselves understood to be conferred on things *by* some arbitrating subject. This subject could be God, but it could also be something else, for example, life itself or indeed human beings—hence the notion of creating values. The expression is pretty common nowadays, but it is absurd if it is taken literally: it is just as impossible to create a value as it is to come up with a new primary color to add to the three that our retinas can perceive.

13. The Descent into Voluntarism

For Avicenna, the founder and the first representative of the new ontology, existence is conferred by a Creator-God. Consequently, Being retains the sheen of goodness, since God wants what is good for his creatures. God is indeed the Pure Good itself, and his Providence consists in the act by which this Goodness bestows upon creatures not only existence, but also the highest degree of order and goodness that it can grant them.[3] Avicenna's God is also Love—certainly not in the sense of the God of Saint John (1 John 4:8), but in the sense that he desires himself perfectly and, indirectly, also the ideas of his creatures present in his intellect.[4]

Now, when Avicenna affirmed the contingency of all things other than the Creator, he did so only as a purely logical point of departure. He then immediately integrated this contingency into an overarching necessitarianism. In fact, in Avicenna's thought, God, who "must be" or "needs to be" (*wâjib al-wujûd*) and who is the only *per se* necessary being, ends up making everything else necessary—everything that is *not* him, and which without him would be contingent.

Here we can also discern another decisive philosophical move that was to have far-reaching consequences: the good ended up becoming God's prerogative alone. And even within him, it was thought to be found only in the faculty of his creative will. The good shifted, then, from the realm of being to that of having. It became less what God *is*

3   Avicenna, *Shîfâ (Metaphysics)*, IX, 6, Arabic edition, *op. cit.*, pp. 415, 954.
4   Avicenna, *Rasâ'il (Treatise on Love)*, I. Qum, Bidar, s.d., pp. 377–378.

than something that he *possesses*; even if it is still *in* God, it is so as something that he *has*, not what he *is*, as if he might set it down for a time, or sell it. Just as one would speak of a merchant's goods, *the* Good itself became one of God's "goods" among various others.

Starting in the late Middle Ages, Christian theology was pulled in a voluntaristic direction. This was already the case in the thought of Duns Scotus, according to whom the origin of contingency was to be found in the divine will. The same tendency was even clearer in William of Ockham.[5] This shift influenced the way God's relation to the Good was imagined. Previous thinkers saw a simple identity, namely, that God *is* the supreme Good, though to me it seems more accurate to say that God *is* the good of His creatures. Augustine, in a similar vein, was fond of a Biblical verse that in its Latin translation reads, "for me, holding fast to God is [the] good" (*mihi adhaerere Deo bonum est*) (*Ps* 72:28).[6]

After Scotus and Ockham, more and more theologians held that the relation between God and the Good was located in God's will: God *wants* the good of his creatures. But he himself is not necessarily this good; he wants, in other words, some good for his creatures that he himself is not. Now, not all creatures, as we have seen, have the same relation to the good. In the case of rational creatures God must turn this good, in the way in which they are capable of attaining it, into an explicit act of the will. Their good thus becomes the object of a commandment. Yet the commandment itself cannot simultaneously hold for God, in that he cannot obey himself.

Following the reduction of being to mere existence, the desire to be similarly took on a new aspect. It had long been the desire for Being— i.e. Being *as* and *because it was* convertible with the Good. It became the simple desire to persevere in an existence that had become morally neutral. Running parallel to this shift, and perhaps with some

---

5   See L. Honnefelder, *Scientia transcendens. Die formale Bestimmung der Seiendheit und Realität in der Metaphysik des Mittelalters und der Neuzeit (Duns Scotus – Suárez – Wolff – Kant – Pierce)*. Hamburg, Meiner, 1990, pp. 82–94.

6   See, for example, Augustine, *De natura boni*, I, 1, BA, t. I, p. 440; *id., De moribus ecclesiae catholicae*, I, 16, 26, BA, t. I, p. 176.

subterranean connection to it, was another phenomenon that played out in the development of modern physics, at least in its post-Galilean form, and specifically in the way motion was understood. For Aristotle, motion was how the elements strive toward their natural places, where they would attain their ends, the perfected forms of the kinds of things that they are.[7] After Galileo, physics would conceive of physical bodies as being thrown about by an indefinitely self-perpetuating motion, not directed to some end but simply driven on by inertia.[8]

14. The Contingency of Life

One instance of the contingency of all beings is the contingency of human life. But as the contingency of the particular fact of existence that happens to fall to *us*, it is a case that obviously concerns us quite directly. It is *our* existence, the existence which we experience from within as the experience of *being alive*.

There is an old way of conceiving of life that I should like to consider for a moment. It takes life as something into which we are thrown, without our consenting to it. This can already be found in various metaphors used by authors in ancient times. One of the more recurrent forms, found in both the Epicureans and the Gnostics, is that of a ship-wrecked sailor, a castaway washed up on the sands of an unknown shore.[9] The image was more or less submerged, if you will, during the Middle Ages, but has resurfaced consistently in a thin trickle of

7   See Aristotle, *On the Heavens*, IV, 3, 311a4.
8   This inertial movement never has been nor ever will be observed by anyone. It is an object that one must "grasp with the mind" (*mente concipere*), as Galileo says: *Discorsi e dimostrazioni matematiche intorno a due nuove scienze attenenti alla meccanica ed ai movimenti locali*, 4th day, Beginning; *Le Opere di Galileo Galilei*. National Edition, Florence, Barbera, t. 8 (1909), p. 268.
9   Lucretius, *De natura rerum*, V, 222–224 (*proiectus*). On the Gnostic image, see the references given in my *La Sagesse du monde: Histoire de l'expérience humaine de l'univers*. Paris, Fayard, 1999, Ch. VI, pp. 83–84. English translation by Teresa Lavender Fagan: *The Wisdom of the World: The Human Experience of the Universe in Western Thought*. Chicago, University of Chicago, 2003.

references throughout modernity, probably in reminiscence of Lucretius in authors enamored of classical culture.[10]

The view that life is the result of being cast somewhere by chance returned in force in the first half of the nineteenth century as one of the many powerful images circulating in the Romantic era. Thus, on May 26, 1828, on his own birthday, Pushkin composed a short poem in which he wondered "why this unearned [or vain] and fortuitous gift of life has been given" to him, and why life "by some mysterious destiny" is itself "condemned to death."[11] Ten years later, the same tones could be heard again in France, in the young Flaubert's *Mémoires d'un fou*, according to which man is a "grain of sand thrown by an unknown hand into the infinite."[12] They sounded again in 1843, in Denmark: for Kierkegaard's hero in *Repetition*, being alive is like waking up after a long night of drinking only to find that you have been shanghaied, abducted, and pressed into service on a boat going who knows where.[13] These three writers, independently of each other and writing in quite disparate linguistic contexts, bear witness to a mindset that was quite widespread at the time.

Yet, however common it was, this attitude was at first existential and limited to individuals. But by now it has found a foundation in, for

10 See, for example, Pascal, *Discours sur la condition des grands*, 1, *Œuvres complètes*, ed. L. Lafuma. Paris, Seuil, 1963, p. 366a; see also the fragment of the *Pensées* cited below, p. 55; Fénelon, *Lettres sur la religion*, VI, *Œuvres*, Paris, Didot, 1865, t. I, p. 160ab (I owe this reference to L. Devillairs); Samuel Pufendorf, *De jure naturae et gentium…*, II, 2, "De statu hominum naturali," §2 "Ejus miseria." Oxford, Clarendon Press and H. Milford, 1934, p. 105. G. Vico alludes to this passage in *Scienza nuova* (1 /44), 1, 4, §338, *Opere*, ed. A. Battistini. Milan, Mondadori, 1990, t. I, p. 546.

11 A. Pushkin, *Dar naprasnyi, dar slutchaïny…*, *Sotchineniya*, Paris, YMCA Press, 1991, p. 317a. The death herein evoked is in fact an execution (*kazn'*), not death in general (*smert'*), as in the parallel found in *Ocen'*, VI, 3, *ibid.*, p. 374a.

12 G. Flaubert, *Mémoires d'un fou* (1838), Ch. II, *Œuvres complètes*. Paris, Seuil, t. I, p. 231b; see also chapters X and XX, pp. 237b and 244b.

13 S. Kierkegaard, *Gjentagelsen* (1843), II, 11 October, in *Skrifter*. Copenhagen, Gad, 1997, t. IV, p. 68; French translation by N. Viallaneix, *La Reprise*. Paris, Flammarion, "GF," 1990, p. 144, cited in my *La Sagesse du monde, op. cit.*, p. 246.

example, the philosophy of a certain number of biologists, if not in biology itself. In a book that met with some success in the early 1970s, the French biologist Jacques Monod, winner of the 1965 Nobel Prize for Physiology, presents evolution as the result of "chance and necessity" alone, the Democritean expression that he took for his title. ("Chance," incidentally, may simply be another word for "necessity," replacing the old reference to "Providence".) Monod summarizes the origins of life, and then the development of the human species by natural selection, as follows:

> It was far from inevitable that the universe would give rise to life, nor could the development of the human species be expected from Earth's biosphere. It is as if we got lucky at Monte Carlo. We would be shocked if we won a billion dollars; is it really any wonder that we experience our condition as a rather strange one?[14]

The image must have been chosen more for its rhetorical effect than for its rigor. After all, it is hard to see how chance could be an explanatory principle. But it comes from a work of popular science and not a scientific article, so the clumsy image itself is hardly cause enough to avoid an inquiry into some of the questions it broaches. And, popular science or not, it does express a vision that for many otherwise competent experts passes for philosophy. The fact that it is not philosophy certainly does not stop them from disseminating it as such in the media and likewise to the broader public.

15. Self-Envy

The trouble is that this way of seeing things brings along with it certain sentiments that in turn encourage certain patterns of behavior and ways of life. With this in mind, let us examine the casino metaphor more closely, still taking it just as it is, an image and nothing more. Now I rather

---

14   J. Monod, *Le Hasard et la Nécéssité: Essai sur la philosophie naturelle de la biologie moderne*. Paris, Seuil, 1970, p. 161.

doubt that it is really a feeling of "strangeness," as Monod put it, that comes over us when we see someone *else* win a billion at roulette. How do we honestly feel about someone like this, or about someone who wins the jackpot in the lottery, or in general, about anyone who has had spectacularly good luck? It is hardly positive. We cannot respect him, because there is nothing moral about a stroke of fortune, nor do any skills or achievements give us grounds to admire him, because he really did nothing to deserve what happened to him. The only feeling we might have toward him is *envy*. In Monod's analogy we end up in the winner's shoes, not those of a third-party observer. But however happy one might be at winning, the question will still arise: *why me*? The winner cannot chalk it up to any merit on his own part, since whatever qualities he might pride himself on are themselves nothing but the results of chance. So just as, if anything, we *envy* someone else who wins the lottery, we might well wonder whether contemporary humanity's dominant feeling toward itself—encouraged by the view of human origins that Monod and so many others promote—is not a paradoxical *self-envy*.

This is somewhat difficult to conceive of, but a few analogies may help us. For several decades now, for example, psychiatrists have known of a similar phenomenon among Jews who were lucky enough to survive the Shoah while everyone else in their families was exterminated. Those who escaped that fate were left with survivor's guilt, and in anguish wondered why, for what reason, on account of what merit, they had been spared, even unconsciously blaming themselves.[15] Psychiatrists have also noted the more recent appearance of paralyzing complexes in adolescents who have discovered—whether directly from their parents or by other means—that they were in effect chosen to survive from among other potential brothers and sisters who had not been wanted and who had therefore become victims of abortion. There is no guarantee that this condition will not become the unfortunate rule rather than the exception in our societies.

---

15 See, for example, J. Semprun, *Quel beau dimanche!* Paris, Grasser, 1980: Ch. III, p. 139; Ch. VII, pp. 365, 371, and 374. The psychiatrist Bruno Bettelheim "will not forgive himself [...] for having survived." I owe this reference to Mr. D. Henrici (Munich).

We could pose an analogous question on the level of the whole human race: why should it be the case that it even exists on earth at all—why mankind, rather than some other species? What about all those poor dinosaurs, apparently snuffed out when a meteor struck the planet? Their misfortune, it seems, was to the benefit of mammals, among which were primates and, therefore, eventually humans.

Less dramatically, we might ask why we should be preferred over all the species whose very survival continues to be threatened by the mere presence of man, the most dangerous of all predators, here on Earth. The question is not purely academic. It has become concretely, overwhelmingly urgent in the several decades since the awareness of the human relation to ecological problems first started to prick the conscience of the broader public.

CHAPTER V
Autonomy and Immanence aboard the Modern Ship of State

According to one of Kierkegaard's characters, as we just saw, we find ourselves in the world as if it were a ship that we have boarded without realizing it. Pascal, too, had used the image, albeit discreetly, in the long fragment containing his famous wager: "It is not optional," he says to the freethinker whom he is trying to persuade to take the bet. "You have already committed; you are already aboard" (*vous êtes embarqués*). The same passage even starts out with the motif of the shipwrecked cast-away: "Our soul has been cast into the body."[1]

16. We Are All in the Same Boat

Being in this condition, we are, as they say, "all in the same boat"; and since we are already on board we had better get our act together. Naval officers tend, as a general rule, to have exquisite manners. Far be it from me to belittle their merit in this regard, but one must admit that they simply cannot survive without them. When you are condemned to live for weeks, even months on end trapped on a ship with people whose company you have not exactly chosen, you have compelling reasons for trying to avoid any possible grounds for friction. Rules become urgent necessities.

The image of the ship as a representation of the human community took on dimensions that one could very well call metaphysical in the

---

1 "Notre âme est *jetée* dans le corps." Pascal, *Pensées*, §233, ed. L. Brunschvicg. Paris, Hachette, 1925, t. II, pp. 146 and 141.

writings of Joseph Conrad, the great English author of Polish origin, who was himself an officer in the British merchant marine. All of his works are rich illustrations of this metaphor, but it is particularly striking in one of his very first tales, *The Nigger of the 'Narcissus'* (1897). The titular black sailor on the ship *Narcissus* is ill, but he is also adept at manipulating the compassion of others. His presence poisons the whole atmosphere to such an extent that a mutiny breaks out, pitting the officers against the ordinary sailors. But then the vessel lists hard and begins to capsize, bobbing perilously on her flank for a whole night. It takes the efforts of the entire crew to right her again before it is too late. The crew here should be understood as a small-scale image of the city, with its men of honor but also its free-riding profiteers and its rebels. Conversely, dry land itself appears on the horizon at the end of the story like some sort of enormous ship.[2] Conrad gives us a key hint at the beginning, when the *Narcissus* first sets sail: the sea is "as empty as the sky."[3] We humans have no point of reference at all—neither here below, nor in some heavenly world high above—that can help us to orient ourselves. We have to get by on our own, literally "with the means we have on board."

17. Autonomy

This is precisely the kind of situation underlying our notion of *autonomy*, one of the watchwords of the modern project. Taking the term beyond its original, juridical sense, political philosophy in the modern era applies it to the ordering of human life in general to denote a process of *self*-organization.

Modern reflections on the origins of human institutions tend to imagine the development of civilization as a whole as the story of a progressive movement from one model of interpersonal relations to another: from *status* to *contract*. Statuses are inherited at birth; contracts emerge from negotiations between agents capable of entering such agreements.

---

2   J. Conrad, *The Nigger of the Narcissus*, V, ed. D. Bone. Oxford, Oxford University Press, "World's Classics," 1961, p. 170.

3   *Ibid.*, pp. 33, 35.

This view of history provided the framework, for example, for the English legal historian Sir Henry Sumner Maine's classic and influential study on ancient law.[4]

In the conception of modern political philosophy, it was in a time and place far beyond the reach of prehistorians that the primal act establishing human society occurred. It is of course postulated only in theory and never verified as an actual event. And this act is conceived precisely as the conclusion of a contract for society. Thanks to the title of Rousseau's famous treatise, the term "social contract" is now well known. But well before him it was already prefigured in the medieval notion of a pact existing implicitly between subjects and their king, whom it obliges to fulfill certain responsibilities toward his people. It was perhaps in the work of the German monk Manegold of Lautenbach (†1103) that the idea first appeared. Manegold used it to argue against the rival notion, developing concurrently, that kings derived a divine right to rule directly from God such that they did not need to answer to anyone but him.[5]

In the seventeenth century, the notion of the contract became central to political philosophy through the work of Thomas Hobbes, who took it as the basis of his argument for the legitimacy of absolute monarchy. In a way he stood in continuity with the medieval tradition of contract theory. But he broke with that tradition in that he never referred to an historical, datable contract, nor to a concrete king and people. Instead, he posited a primordial contract—drawn up and concluded in a distant past far beyond anything within the bounds of history—as the origin of the polis.[6] Rousseau, for his part, took the idea of the contract so far that he saw it as the constitutive principle of society as such. Hobbes supposed that human society already existed, or at any rate existed to a sufficient extent that its primal act might be to place itself in the sovereign's hands. Rousseau, though, saw the contract as a way for society to act

4   H.J.S. Maine, *Ancient Law*, ed. J.H. Morgan, London, Dent, 1960, Ch. IX, p. 182; see also Ch. X, p. 218.
5   Manegold of Lautenbach, *Liber ad Gebehardum*, §30, MG Lib. Lit., t. I, p. 365, and §§47–48, pp. 391–392.
6   T. Hobbes, *Leviathan*, II, 17, ed. M. Oakeshott. Oxford, Blackwell, 1960, p. 112.

upon itself in a more fundamental way. Society has to use the contract in order to constitute itself *as* society before it is even capable of making any other decision, e.g. whether to give itself a king. The "social contract" is precisely this act by which society moves toward its own constitution. Through it, each would-be participant abandons the rights that he has by nature as an individual, but he does so in order to regain them in a new form as a member of the social body.

The social contract as Rousseau explained it was located on a much deeper level than it was for the thinkers who had preceded him, since for Rousseau it brought about nothing less than the movement from animality to humanity. In the Hobbesian version, it is true, a new man emerged through the contract, but there the idea remained implicit.[7] In Rousseau's, however, we find the striking words: "The passage from the state of nature to the civil state produces a very remarkable change *in man*, by substituting justice for instinct in his conduct and giving his actions the morality they had formerly lacked." It is this change that makes "an intelligent being, *a man*, out of a stupid and unimaginative animal."[8]

18. The Immanent Society

A society constituted in this way—self-constituted, strictly speaking—is a social space that is essentially closed in on itself. The presence of an external element would spoil everything. We can see this above all in today's democratic societies. They take shape as a *flat* social space: from the start, no one is supposed to be above anybody else. But its flatness also leaves the democratic social space closed. Indeed, it has to be closed in order to be flat. Anything beyond its bounds and extrinsic to its order has to be kept out, above all anything from what we might call the Great Beyond, or whatever claims to have any intrinsic worth or essential importance *in itself* rather than receiving its value as a result of

7   See D. Negro, *El mito del hombre nuevo*. Madrid, Encuentro, 2009, pp. 66, 77.

8   J.-J. Rousseau, *Du contrat social*, I, 8, *Œuvres complètes*, eds. R. Dérathé *et al.* Paris, Gallimard, "Bibliothèque de la Pléiade," 1964, t. III, p. 364. My emphasis. English translation by G.D.H. Cole, modified.

democratic consensus. The democratic social space has to remain within itself—it has to be, in Latin, *immanens*, whence of course comes our word "immanent". Tocqueville observed that aristocratic man constantly had his attention turned to something that was outside of himself.[9] Democratic man, on the other hand, is entirely self-referential.

An anecdote will illustrate this nicely, even if its historical veracity is not entirely certain. In 1787, the American Constitutional Convention was at a standstill, with the delegates unable to agree on an important point. When Benjamin Franklin proposed that they open the sessions with prayer in order to overcome the impasse, and that they appoint chaplains to this end, Alexander Hamilton allegedly scoffed that he did not see any need for "foreign aid."[10]

There is another image of fundamental significance for modern political philosophy that brilliantly conveys the sense of modern society's self-enclosure. It depicts social life as a game, and society as a group of people playing it—for example, a card game, its players seated around a tidy table of smooth green felt. The game image appeared for the first time in Hobbes and showed up again in Adam Smith, who also spoke of "the great chess-board of human society."[11] It is at the basis of John Rawls' theory of justice, in which a very conscious fiction is used to construct a starting situation analogous to that of card players being dealt their hands.[12] Yet, if new players keep coming into the hall and sitting down at the table, the game, with all its rules agreed on prior to their arrival, simply cannot get underway: it has to start over, possibly with the rules re-negotiated.

---

9   A. de Tocqueville, *De la démocratie en Amérique*, II, 2, 2, ed. A. Jardin. Paris, Gallimard, "Bibliothèque de la Pléiade," 1992, p. 613.

10 See *The Records of the Federal Convention of 1787*, ed. M. Farrand. New Haven, Yale University Press, 1937, t. I, pp. 450–452; see also t. III, pp. 470–473; 499; and t. V, p. 531 (*non vidi*).

11 T. Hobbes, *Leviathan*, II, 30, *op. cit.*, p. 227; Adam Smith, *A Theory of Moral Sentiments*, VI, 2, 2, 17, eds. D.D. Raphael and A.L. Macfie. Oxford, Clarendon Press, 1976, p. 234.

12 J. Rawls, *A Theory of Justice*, IX, §79. Cambridge (Mass.), Belknap, 1971, pp. 525–526, 527, on the image of the game; on his intention to develop and to generalize the idea of the social contract, see I, §3, p. 11.

This fiction is of great didactic value when it comes to understanding how society functions, or how it should do so. But it does not correspond in the least to our concrete situation. Humanity, as a species of animal, can of course only keep existing precisely if it replaces the dead with new living members of the same kind. To stick with our image, humanity doesn't put the game on hold to let new players sit down at the table as others slip away. For it to continue existing—to continue *being*—it has to produce more Being by making new *beings*, human beings. And we humans ourselves are, of course, the ones who have to do this.

19. Nothing Is Easy

But do things necessarily have to go on that way? There is another side to the project of autonomy. Modernity supposes that the highest human ideal is self-determination. But why should *being* be the object of our self-determination? Why not *non-being* instead? Leibniz, after posing his famous question, "Why is there something rather than nothing?" adds this curious explanation for why the matter is not self-evident, and why the question is worth asking: non-being, he says, is "simpler and easier than something."[13]

We could have a bit of fun along these lines with a comparative review of life and death from a purely economic perspective, a cost/benefit analysis, as it were. I should like to invite you, then, to join me in a little exercise in dark humor. Here is what I would say: from this purely economic perspective, committing suicide would be much more profitable than staying alive. At least it would be "simpler and easier," to borrow Leibniz's expression, than anything else we might try to do to ourselves. To improve our physical appearance even the slightest bit we have to shed blood, sweat, and tears working out at the gym, or putting in long hours at the beauty salon, and we have to avoid all sorts of good things while we are at it. As for growth in virtue, it takes year after year of sustained effort. In both cases, we end up with rather modest results, always precarious, fragile, and endangered. On the other hand, suicide allows

13   G. Leibniz, *Principes de la nature et de la grâce*, §7, ed. A. Robinet. Paris, PUF, 1954, p. 45.

us not only to attain a radical and almost instantaneous transformation, but also to do it relatively cheaply and easily. Moreover, there is no risk of relapse. There's something solid and definitive about it.

I realize that this sort of pleasantry can get a bit tiresome, but the philosophical question that suicide poses is a serious one. It is to this that we shall turn next.

CHAPTER VI
Suicide and the Love of Life

Suicide is a philosophical question, but is it just one among many? Albert Camus thought otherwise. He began the 1942 essay that catapulted him to fame overnight with a sentence that was to become almost proverbial: "There is only one really serious philosophical question, and that is suicide."[1] Camus, in truth more of a writer than a philosopher, was looking for a shocking line, and he found a good one here. Yet in spite of the waves he made with his claim, the problem is much older than Camus.

20. Suicide

Already in antiquity various thinkers debated the moral status of suicide. But it is true that they considered this question as merely one ethical problem among many others. It was certainly not seen as the only serious one.

Things took a new turn with Schopenhauer. Although *The World as Will and Representation* dates back to 1818, during the period of the Restoration, he only really became popular in the 1850s. In the years thereafter, however, his influence on the European intelligentsia would be difficult to overestimate. Most professional philosophers, to be sure, did not take him terribly seriously. Schopenhauer himself was not particularly friendly to them, either. But between the middle of the nineteenth century and the Great War just about every single artist, writer, painter, musician, and so on in all of Europe felt his influence. Many of them adopted his worldview, sometimes passionately, and it left its mark on

---

1   A. Camus, *Le Mythe de Sisyphe*, *Essais*, eds. R. Quilliot and L. Faucon. Paris, Gallimard, "Bibliothèque de la Pléiade," 1965, pp. 89–211, esp. p. 99.

their works well into the twentieth century.[2] Among those philosophers who were sympathetic to Schopenhauer was Eduard von Hartmann, who, although rather (and perhaps rightly) forgotten today, managed to popularize a vulgar version of Schopenhauer's worldview with his book *Philosophy of the Unconscious* (1869). Today nobody takes that work seriously, but it enjoyed tremendous success up until the 1920s.[3] Even the young Vladimir Soloviev, for example, wrote of it in his 1874 doctoral thesis as the latest great achievement of Western philosophy.

The fundamentally decisive move in Schopenhauer's thought concerns the will. Traditionally the will had been defined as a faculty that had reason present within it, enabling its subject to choose the good. It was the presence of reason that also distinguished it from blind desire.[4] But Schopenhauer posited a radical division between reason and the will.[5] Consequently, the will to live became nothing but a blind force indifferent to the good. Being, for living things, was conceived as the *mere fact of being alive*—the last stage of the reduction of Being to existence[6]—and was itself decoupled from the good. One of Schopenhauer's most enthusiastic disciples, Philipp Mainländer, explicitly inverted Aristotle's affirmation of the superiority of being over nothingness in his assertion that the highest principle of all morality lies in "the will, inflamed by the knowledge that non-being is better than being."[7] It should be noted that Mainländer followed his ideas to their logical conclusion: he took his own life the day after his book's publication.

2   See A. Henry (ed.), *Schopenhauer et la création littéraire en Europe*. Paris, Klincksieck, 1989; on Beckett and Borges, see D.E. Wellberry, *Schopenhauers Bedeutung für die moderne Literatur*. Munich, Siemens Stiftung, 1998.

3   E. von Hartmann, *Philosophie des Unbewußten: Versuch einer Weltanschauung*. Berlin, Duncker, 1869. Twelve new editions had been published by 1923.

4   See above, §11, pp. 28–29.

5   A. Schopenhauer, *Über den Willen in der Natur, Werke, op. cit.*, t. III, p. 339.

6   See above, §12, pp. 30–32.

7   P. Mainländer, *Philosophie der Erlösung* (1876), in the anthology *Vom Verwesen der Welt und anderen Restposten*, ed. U. Horstmann. Recklinghausen, Manuscriptum, 2003, p. 85.

As for Schopenhauer, the practical attitude that he advocated and had the courage to practice in his own personal life is what the ancients called "encratism": continence, or the rejection of marriage, and above all of procreation.

But Schopenhauer had some very hard words to say about suicide properly speaking. Suicide, he held, would only lead to an illusory liberation. Far from silencing the will to live, suicide amounts to a final demonstration of its hold on us: the would-be suicide actually *wants* life, it is just that he is dissatisfied with the terms on which it is offered to him. Suicide is in fact a preeminent act of the will, whereas it is precisely the will that ought to be negated. All that suicide can succeed in suppressing is a singular and fleeting manifestation of the will: the body. The will's essence is left untouched.[8]

21. Suicide and Immortality

It was in a cultural atmosphere tinged with Schopenhauer's thought that Dostoyevsky, too, considered the problem of suicide. Moreover, at that time—that is, in the 1860s—a wave of suicides both real and imagined was sweeping across Russia. In his *Diary of a Writer*, he starts by mentioning a few in particular, especially that of the liberal publicist Alexander Herzen's daughter, whose suicide was all over the papers. Now, Dostoyevsky was a brilliant novelist. He must not be judged as a philosopher, in which role he was really not quite at ease. You can search him in vain for rigorous arguments. On the other hand, his insights are priceless. Precisely since he was a novelist above all else, he puts forth his reflections in this *Diary* entry in fictitious form, imagining a suicide note written by an atheist (or as he says, "materialist"). This imaginary materialist explains that he has decided to put an end to his life for no particular reason at all—just out of pure boredom (*skuka*).[9]

---

8 A. Schopenhauer, *Die Welt als Wille und Vorstellung*, IV, §69, *op. cit.*, t. I., pp. 541–543.

9 F.M. Dostoyevsky, *Dnevnik pisatelya*, 1876, October, I, 4, *Sotchineniya*, t. XIII. St. Petersburg, Nauka, 1994, pp. 321–322; French translation by G. Aucouturier. Paris, Gallimard, 1972, pp. 725–728.

Strange though it may seem, that was not an entirely isolated posture in the literature of that era. It would resurface, for example, in Martin Decoud, one of the lesser characters in what is perhaps Joseph Conrad's finest novel, *Nostromo*. Decoud ultimately kills himself out of "want of faith in himself and others." Finding himself stranded, alone, and idle, he loses, along with the life of action that he had been living, the long-harbored illusion of an independent existence, and he drowns "in the immense indifference of things."[10]

Dostoyevsky's suicide note was inspired by ideas from Schopenhauer, its desperate (if fictitious) author echoing, for example, Schopenhauer's critique of Leibnizian optimism. With what right, he asks, did nature make me? The consciousness that it gave me is the source of suffering. The life of each individual, like that of the species, is doomed to nothingness in the end. The sacrifices of generations past and present for the sake of some kind of hypothetical future human happiness are just as repulsive and unacceptable as an individual's sacrifice for the harmony of the whole. Accordingly, the suicidal author says he imagines life as a laboratory experiment (*proba*) conducted to figure out whether beings made like humans can really endure life. But we are not told who the mad scientist running the experiment might be—worse, it turns out that there is no one running the experiment after all, no one to hold responsible for it. The author thus decides to condemn nature itself to death, or at least that part of nature over which he has such authority—namely, himself.

Many readers took the sneering apologist as a mouthpiece for Dostoyevsky's own thoughts and were duly outraged. He was obliged to return to the subject, this time speaking in his own name and listing a number of theses that he himself genuinely held but, he admitted explicitly, could not be proved by any argument.

He pushed these basic tenets of his rather forcefully. Above all, it is the conviction that the soul exists and is immortal that is, in Dostoyevsky's view, indispensable. Without this faith man's own existence

10 J. Conrad, *Nostromo: A Tale of the Seaboard* (1904), III, 10, ed. M. Seymour Smith. London, Penguin Classics, 1988, pp. 412–416; on the theory of action implied here, see I, 6, p. 86.

is unnatural, unbearable, and intolerable. The immortality of the soul is in fact the loftiest idea that humans can have. All our other noble thoughts derive from it, even the love of humanity is not possible without it. Ultimately, "suicide—once the idea of immortality has been lost—becomes an absolute necessity, indeed an inevitability for anyone who in his own intellectual development has raised himself even the slightest bit above the level of beasts." The belief in immortality, on the other hand, with its promise of eternal life, paradoxically binds man all the more tightly to life on earth.[11]

But neither Dostoyevsky nor Camus took the inquiry far enough. First, one might legitimately raise two very sensible objections to Dostoyevsky's claims, as indeed some have already done. For one, the great majority of mankind—including many quite intelligent folks—keep on living until they die of old age, or at any rate of some cause other than suicide. This fact amounts to a kind of quotidian plebiscite, deciding daily in favor of the goodness of life: if people judge life evil and think death preferable to it, why do not they kill themselves?[12] Yet many people cope very well with the idea that with their death it will all be over; the loss of faith in the soul's immortality is thus not as serious as some would have us believe.[13]

What was missing from these considerations actually comes up briefly and in a particularly clear way in Camus. He opened the right door in his essay by raising what he thought was the fundamental question (i.e. the question of suicide, allegedly the most important in philosophy), but only to close it immediately once again by saying: "To decide

11 F.M. Dostoyevsky, *Dnevnik pisatelya...*, December, I, *op. cit.*, 3, pp. 387–391, citation from p. 390; French translation, pp. 810–815, citation (modified) from p. 815.

12 See Epicurus, *Letter to Menoeceus*, §§126–127, and more recently H. Bergson, *Les Deux Sources de la morale et de la religion*. Paris, Alcan, 1932, p. 277. Bergson seems to be aiming above all at Schopenhauer.

13 See, for example, L. Strauss, "Zur Ideologie des politischen Zionismus (In Erwiderung auf drei Aufsätze Max Josephs)," in *Gesammelte Schriften*, t. I, *Die Religionskritik Spinozas und zugehörige Schriften*, ed. H. Meier. Stuttgart/Weimar, Metzler, 2008, 3rd expanded ed., p. 447. Strauss refers explicitly to this passage from Dostoyevsky.

whether or not life is worth living is to answer the fundamental question in philosophy." The line was meant to make his initial claim explicit. But this is actually a dramatic narrowing of the question. Dostoyevsky implicitly, and Camus quite explicitly, were only asking themselves whether life was worth *living*.

For my part, though, I would argue that the real question is whether life is worth *giving*.

22. The Love of Living and the Love of Life

We speak too easily of a "love of life." I would propose that we distinguish a "love of *living*" from a love of life, and I would move toward this distinction by taking a cue from one of St. Augustine's reflections. At one point in the *Confessions* he addresses a very interesting question: why does St. John does say in his Gospel that there are people who "hate the light" (John 3:20)? And why does one of Terence's characters say that "truth begets hatred" (*veritas parit odium*)? Would it not be more natural for people to love the light and the truth, since they are unquestionably good things? Augustine's answer draws a distinction between two kinds of truth, deploying a very telling phrase to do so: "They love the truth when it enlightens, and they hate it when it reproves" (*amant eam lucentem, oderunt eam redarguentem*).[14] Truth may be *lucens*, in which case we like it; but it may also be *redarguens*, in which case we avoid it and even wish it did not exist—which is to say that we hate it. The first truth is like a lamp illuminating the things that we want to see in order to be able to act upon them, use them, consume them, etc.

For the second sort of truth, Augustine uses a word that is very difficult to translate from the Latin. The verb's root evokes brilliance and light, as in the lustrous metal *argentum*, silver. The prefix *re-* indicates something's repetition or return to itself or its source. The French translators of the

14 Augustine, *Confessiones*, X, 23, 34, BA, t. XIV, pp. 202–204. English translation by E.B. Pusey. Heidegger noted the significance of this passage; see his1921 summer semester course on "Augustinus und der Neuplatonismus," in *Gesamtausgabe*, Frankfurt, Klostermann, t. LX, 1995, p. 201; even clearer is O. Pöggeler, *Der Denkweg Martin Heideggers*. Pfullingen, Neske, 1963, pp. 38–39 and 116.

Bibliothèque augustinienne render the verb as *accuser*, which in addition to the meanings of the English *accuse* can also mean *to show, to make appear, to emphasize, to bring out*—as we say in French that light "accuses" shadows when it grows brighter. As long as these other meanings are understood, and not just the sense of leveling blame for some transgression, *accuser* seems to me to be an excellent choice in French. Truth is the light that we can shine upon things we want to know, and it gives us mastery over them; but it can also flash back at us and bring out into the open all the dirty little secrets that we would prefer to leave hidden. We covet truth in the former mode, but we flee from it in the latter. If we really love truth as such we should want it to shed all of its light on us, too.

We can apply the same distinction to other fields as well. Take, for example, our relationship with nature. We like it when it serves us as a resource we can exploit or a landscape we can hike over. But we hate it when it limits us and imposes its own norms on us from within our bodies (which is why we sometimes speak dismissively or even scornfully of biological issues).[15]

Or take our relation to time, looking in either direction. We love the past when it serves as an exotic landscape for our adventures in historical tourism, but we hate it insofar as it stamps us with a particular identity. We love the future when it serves as a playground for our utopian dreams of paradise on earth, but we hate it insofar as our responsibilities toward it might force us to take rigorous measures in the present in order to leave it livable for our descendants.

The distinction between the two ways of viewing truth—its modes of enlightening and reproving—is also relevant for the problem of life and human existence that concerns us here. Nowadays the expression "love of life" is used rather indiscriminately. You can scarcely make it through a eulogy, even in cases of suicide, without tripping over the nearly ritualistic phrase: "He/She loved life" . In light of the distinction that I have just drawn, one might well say: to love *living*, to be glad that one is alive, is not properly speaking to love *life*, but rather to love *enjoying* life, namely, to love your *own* life. And thus basically it is to love only yourself.

15 See above, §6, pp. 14–16.

In this case we must still ask a serious question. Each of us should ask: Do I really love life insofar as it is life? Or just insofar as it is *mine*? An example may help to make clear that this question is anything but frivolous. Take justice. Loving justice is not the same thing as demanding that other people do justice to *me*. The attitude needed for the latter is not very difficult to master. But to practice the first consistently, you need to be very nearly a *virtuoso* of virtue. If we loved justice for itself, we would wish justice to be done even when it is to our detriment.

Now, then, there is nothing particularly magical about the love of living, the love of being alive, since we are in any case already "all aboard." It is enough just to let it happen. Loving *life*, though, in the strict sense of the expression, means loving it when it is not our own.

To do so, it is not enough to promote or even to practice respect for life. To be sure, allowing human lives to continue once they are already being lived is a very important first step—and one that is not always so convenient for us to take. But one could say that we just have to get used to whatever lives are already here since, to draw on the metaphor once again, we are all in the same boat.

Loving life, though, means something more. It means loving it when its very existence depends on us. Loving life means *giving* life. But why should we?

CHAPTER VII
The Self-Destruction of the Human Race

Earlier I mentioned that in late modernity we find a mistrust and even a hatred for metaphysics.[1] One very effective way to put an end to metaphysics—admittedly, perhaps a tad *too* effective—would simply be for humanity to destroy itself.

23. Putting an End to the Metaphysical Animal

If it is true that we humans are metaphysical animals, then by our very nature we cannot help engaging in metaphysics, or something like it. Nietzsche was commenting on the same phenomenon when he said that as long as we have grammar we will have theology, too: "I am afraid that we are not rid of God because we still believe in grammar" (*Ich fürchte, wir werden Gott nicht los, weil wir noch an die Grammatik glauben*).[2] Grammar is precisely our species' capacity for language, raised to the level of conscious consideration: it is our reflection on our very way of being, which is to say on being endowed with *logos*. To put an end to grammar we would have to eliminate what makes us human, the same thing that makes us metaphysical animals. And, naturally, if humanity should someday be destroyed any subsequent possibility of metaphysics would also be killed in the cradle.

Now, the question of humanity's self-destruction is no longer a purely theoretical one. It has become a very concrete possibility. For want of better ones at the moment, there are currently three principal

---

1   See above, §§5–6, pp. 11–16.
2   F. Nietzsche, *Götzen-Dämmerung*, "Die 'Vernunft' in der Philosophie," 5, *KSA*, t. VI, p. 78.

ways it might come about: environmental devastation, nuclear war, and demographic extinction.

"Better" means of our species' self-destruction, still to be perfected, might come through developments in biotechnology that would someday allow us to transcend humanity. I am not qualified to say whether this is a realistic possibility or merely a pipe dream. But, feasible or not, it is at least interesting to consider the idea of this kind of transcendence, especially since it has been around for as long as it has—since long before anything like the technical means for its hypothetical realization could have been in place. The most brilliant expression of the idea is probably the bold declaration uttered by Nietzsche's Zarathustra: "Man is something that must be overcome" (*Der Mensch ist etwas, das überwunden werden soll*).[3] This thought becomes even more interesting when we recall that, all things considered, the claim came just a short time—four centuries at most—after the great Renaissance authors had issued their treatises extolling the dignity of man, and an even shorter time—two and a half centuries—after Bacon's and Descartes' slogans promoting man's domination of nature had first caught on. In Nietzsche's wake notions like anti-humanism, transhumanism, and post-humanism have been crowding the public square. Anti-humanism, for one, may have first appeared in a 1919 lecture by the Russian poet Aleksandr Blok, under the title "The Shipwreck of Humanism."[4] And transhumanism was coined in 1957 by the British biologist and high-ranking official Julian Huxley (the novelist Aldous Huxley's brother), who at the height of his career had been the first secretary general of UNESCO.[5]

But just what kind of man is it that we are supposed to overcome, to break with? My answer would be: not necessarily with man as the lord and master of nature, but certainly with man as the metaphysical animal

3   F. Nietzsche, *Also sprach Zarathustra*, Prologue, 3, *KSA*, t. IV, p. 14. The expression occurs several times in this work, sometimes with *sollen* (implying "moral obligation"), and sometimes with *müssen* ("necessity," as in "physical necessity").

4   Aleksandr Blok, "Krushênie gumanizma," in *Iskusstvo I revoliutsiya*. Moscow, Sovremmenik, 1979, pp. 288–308; cf. §3, p. 291, and §7, p. 306.

5   J.S. Huxley, *New Bottles for New Wine. Essays*. London, Chatto & Windus, 1957, p. 17.

constantly yearning for a transcendence of a non-biotechnological sort. Nietzsche understood this very well. For him, it was in and through the Superman (*Übermensch*) that man was to be overcome. Though he flirted for a time with phrasing heavily influenced by Darwinism, then beginning to inundate the intellectual world, he took care to distance himself from it by the end of his conscious life.[6] Nietzsche's Superman does not belong to some race or species superior to humans on the great scale of being. Instead, he is the human being who turns his back on heaven, remains entirely faithful to the earth, and accepts the ultimate consequences of his absolute fidelity. Above all else this consists in embracing the "eternal return of the same," the highest affirmation of immanence, and one which implies the radical impossibility of any escape.[7]

Whether or not contemporary thought makes reference to Nietzsche, it may be that it is heading in the same direction. And it may be that the old aversion to metaphysics is quietly changing into a loathing for the concrete locus of the concern for metaphysics—namely, into a loathing for man himself. If so, then the aim, quite simply, should be to get it over with and put an end to the whole species.

24. The Tools for the Job

Here I would like to speak only of the means by which it *currently* seems possible for humanity's self-destruction to play out. After all, according to Hegel, whom I shall stand with here (*si parvum licet componere magno*), the philosopher's task is to consider the present rather than to speculate about the future. Now in the previous section I listed three ways in which we might destroy ourselves.[8] They became possible in succession, and they have all been at our disposal for several decades now.

First, since the onset of the Industrial Age humans have been releasing toxic wastes into the environment that are difficult for the planet to

6 F. Nietzsche, *Der Antichrist*, §3, *KSA*, t. VI, p. 170; see also Fragments 11 (413), November 1887–March 1888, *KSA*, t. XIII, p. 191, and 15 (120), Spring 1888, *ibid.*, p. 481.

7 F. Nietzsche, *Also sprach Zarathustra*, I, "Von der schenkenden Tugend," 2, *KSA*, t. IV, p. 99.

8 See above, §23, pp.54–55.

break down, compromising not only our comfort but also, perhaps, our very survival. We have been destroying natural safeguards without being able to replace them, and in so doing we have been threatening the regularity of the climate. And our habits of consumption have been exhausting the various kinds of non-renewable energy sources on which we are dependent. Though the environmental problem began long ago, our awareness of it only goes back to the 1960s or no.

Next, since the invention of atomic weapons in the 1940s and their progressive refinement thereafter, mankind has had the means to achieve total self-destruction in a spectacular conflagration, and to do so actively, deliberately, simply by pushing a button.

Finally, since the 1960s advances in mechanical and chemical contraception have given mankind the ability to destroy itself little by little, in a discreet, passive extinction, perhaps without even realizing it, just by ceasing to reproduce.

Philosophers have reacted with an understandable delay to the first two dangers, but ultimately rather weakly and with divergent interests. Some, like Karl Jaspers and Günther Anders, addressed the atomic bomb.[9] Hans Jonas, in his 1979 book *The Imperative of Responsibility*, considers the ecological crisis on the basis of the biological turn in his thought.[10] Since then, environmentalism has been a fashionable theme, so much so that it has grown rather worn out by now.

The demographic danger has had rather less luck. Some philosophers, it is true, have reflected on the duties that the present generation owes to those to come, and some of these have even had some very insightful things to say on the subject. When Hans Jonas looked at the bond between generations, for example, he took the image of a nursing infant as paradigmatic for the notion of responsibility: the infant's very existence amounts to an appeal, its *is* implies an *ought*.[11] But on demographic questions he remained enthralled to the illusion of

9   K. Jaspers, *Die Atombombe und die Zukunft des Menschen*. Munich/Zürich, 1957; G. Anders, *Die andere Drohung. Radikale Überlegungen zum atomaren Zeitalter*. Munich, C.H. Beck, 1993, 6th ed.

10   H. Jonas, *Das Prinzip Verantwortung. Versuch einer Ethik für die technologische Zivilisation*. Frankfurt, Insel, 1979.

11   *Ibid.*, pp. 234–242.

overpopulation that dominated his generation.[12] A little later, Dieter Birnbacher published a deservedly successful book on the responsibility we bear toward future generations.[13]

On the other hand, people rarely consider the very simple fact that the existence of these hypothetical future generations depends entirely on the will of the present generation. Few philosophers, whether real or so-called, have undertaken any sustained reflection on the possibility of the demographic extinction of the human race. I know of only one, a Frenchman by the name of Christian Godin. Incidentally, he claimed that, far more than possible, humanity's demographic extinction is probable, not to say downright inevitable. In his treatment of the concrete causes as well as the psychological reasons that he believes are going to bring it about, he also highlighted, and rightly so, the silent role of the corporate world in all of this.[14]

25. The Burden on Each Generation

Paleontologists have different ways of determining when the human species first arose from earlier hominids. The criteria they look for vary: the practice of funerary rites, the use of tools, the awareness of time, etc. But whatever the criterion one uses, humanity's journey has already spanned hundreds of thousands of years at the very least. The five thousand years of history marked by the invention and use of writing seem little more than a fleeting instant in comparison. Some biologists think that each species, from the moment it enters the great game of life on earth is determined to survive for only a certain amount of time thereafter before going extinct. They also tend to add that humanity could still live quite a while, supposedly being at a stage of its development corresponding to puberty in the life of the individual. On this view, humanity is undergoing its adolescent crisis.

12 *Ibid.*, pp. 252 ("demographic explosion") and 338. See also pp. 272, 274, 323, 328–332, 336, and 340.
13 D. Birnbacher, *Verantwortung für zukünftige Generationen*. Stuttgart, Reclam, 1988. The author also takes the overpopulation hypothesis as a background assumption; see p. 139.
14 C. Godin, *La Fin de l'humanité*. Seyssel, Champ Vallon, 2003, p. 15.

We need not concern ourselves with the rigor of that analogy. What we can say is that the realization of any future for humanity, adulthood or not, will depend on each successive generation's will to reproduce. This also means that it is dependent on a choice that is less and less implicit—or, if you will, more and more explicit, deliberate, and consciously considered. The fact that we have made it hundreds of thousands of years so far in no way implies that our adventure will continue. It really is completely dependent on the present generation. However immense the duration of the human experience has been, the whole thing hangs on what is just a very fine point in comparison to that vast span.

As for the mere fact of the matter, it is obvious and has been well known for a long while now: it would suffice for us to agree to stop reproducing and humanity would just disappear. The oldest philosophical mention of it that I have been able to find comes from a biblical commentary by Levi ben Gershom (known as Gersonides), a Jewish-Provençal philosopher and astronomer active in the first half of the fourteenth century (d. 1344).[15] But such considerations could also be found in the theological polemics for and against virginity in the Patristic period. Those who chose the monastic life, and thus celibacy, were sometimes confronted with the objection that their way of life could not be generalized since humanity would disappear if everyone did as they were doing. They responded that their goal was a new way of life, a heavenly way of life, in which there was simply no need at all for corporeal fertility.[16]

Some have even calculated how much time without reproducing it would take for the process to become irreversible, sixty years being the common estimate. That figure can already be found in the second part of the *Roman de la Rose*, which Jean de Meung finished composing around 1280.[17] In a famous sonnet, Shakespeare would later insist to his young friend, who was perhaps also his lover, that he should get married and

---

15 See for example Gersonides, *Commentary on the Torah*, t. I, *Genesis* (in Hebrew). Jerusalem, Mosad Rav Kook, 1992, p. 47.

16 See for example Gregory of Nyssa, *On Virginity*, ch. XIII, *PG*, t. XLVI, col. 376D–381B.

17 Jean de Meung, *Le Roman de la Rose*, v. 19583–19598, ed. D. Poirion. Paris, Flammarion, "GF," 1974, p. 519.

have children, since without marriage and reproduction humanity would be brought to nothing: "[T]hreescore year would make the world away."[18]

Let us note, then, a fact that is at once amusing and sobering: at any given moment, humanity as a whole has in some sense roughly the same life expectancy as the youngest of its individual members.

26. Collective Suicide

If the demographic crisis is well known in terms of its statistical realities, it also affords us the conceptual advantage, if one may call it as much, of taking the problem of suicide to another level. Prior to this crisis the complexity of the discussion of suicide was chiefly due to certain, shall we say, *nuisances* that anyone who committed it had to deal with, and which I omitted from my earlier appraisal in terms of input and output.[19] The would-be suicide at least has the courage to take these nuisances upon himself, and upon himself alone, and forces them on no one else. It is this, incidentally, that makes suicide a moral paradox that must be acknowledged, difficult though it be to admit: suicide holds together qualities that everywhere else are irreconcilable, for it is the only act that is *simultaneously* reprehensible and respectable, noble without being good.[20]

It's more difficult to conceive of a collective suicide on the part of the entire human race. Some philosophers have nonetheless raised the possibility—John Stuart Mill, for example, who credited the idea to Novalis.[21] Mill only mentioned it in passing, but today we ought to consider it in more concrete terms and with greater urgency.

18 William Shakespeare, Sonnet 11.
19 See above, §19, pp. 44–45.
20 See Augustine, *De civitate Dei*, I, 22, ed. C.J. Perl. Paderborn, Schöningh, 1979, p. 50.
21 J.S. Mill, *Utilitarianism* (1863), Ch. II, "Utilitarianism, Liberty and Representative Government," ed. A.D. Lindsay. London, Everyman, 1968, p. 12. Mill does not give the reference in Novalis. Probably he means *Hemsterhuis u. Kant-Studien* (1797), *Fragmentblatt*, §20, *Werke, Tagebücher und Briefe*, eds. H.-J. Mähl and R. Samuel. Darmstadt, Wissenschaftliche Buchgesellschaft, 1999, t. II, p. 223.

For nowadays only a small and obsolescent minority still clings to the fantastic illusions of a demographic explosion and planetary overpopulation that were everywhere in the 1960s. By contrast, we hear more and more talk of the "demographic suicide" of Europe—and indeed, in the longer term, of the whole world. As far as I know, the precise expression as such was used for the first time in Raymond Aron's *Memoirs* (1983), appearing there in the very sober, dry style characteristic of that author.[22] But already starting in the 1970s, Pierre Chaunu, a French historian and student of the Braudelian long term, had been sounding the alarm in a rather more dramatic tenor.[23] At the time, Chaunu was met with little more than shrugs or half-pitying sneers. And since then, while it is true that some politicians have used the expression from time to time, they have nonetheless always been careful to avoid proposing any concrete measures in response that might really be able to stop or at the very least slow the demographic decline. A few more serious authors, on the other hand, such as the historian and sometime government official Roland Hureaux, have happily taken a more responsible attitude toward the subject and have added some very practical proposals to their analyses.[24]

I am not qualified to say whether the threat of our species' voluntary extinction is a real one or not. I just mentioned the illusion of overpopulation, and some say that the fear of depopulation is similarly imaginary. Let it suffice to recall that perfectly sober and well-informed authors do indeed take the hypothesis seriously. But basically the reality of the facts of the matter is not a problem for me. Others are better judges here. What interests me is that the hypothesis is plausible even in principle; and in any case given the nature of the issue it can only be verified in the future. Here I simply mean to take this hypothesis as the point of departure for a thought experiment—something that is, after all, a properly philosophical exercise.

22 R. Aron, *Mémoires. 50 ans de réflexion politique*. Paris, Julliard, 1983, p. 750.

23 P. Chaunu, *Le Refus de la vie. Analyse historique du présent*. Paris, Calmann-Lévy, 1975; *id.*, with G. Suffert, *La Peste blanche*. Paris, Gallimard, 1976.

24 R. Hureaux, *Le Temps des derniers hommes. Le devenir de la population dans les sociétés modernes*. Paris, Hachette,

Let us head in that direction, then, and let me end this chapter with the general remark that shifting the ground of the suicide discussion from the level of the individual to that of the species has several other consequences, a few of them advantageous. For one, the act becomes painless, even imperceptible. In the case of "clean" contraception by perfect continence (encratism), there is no cadaver, not even the most microscopic one. There is no identifiable victim, other than the species in general. The act thus becomes innocent.

On the other hand, while the agent is by necessity just as singular as he was in the case of individual suicide, the victim is now an abstract collectivity. The subject and the object of the suicide are no longer identical, so much so that here the word "suicide," etymologically "self-murder," becomes scarcely anything more than a metaphor. And at the same time, with the decoupling of subject and object the act loses the dignity that made it respectable.

CHAPTER VIII
What Right to Life?

Well, who wants to keep the human race going?
P.G. Wodehouse, *Jeeves in the Offing.*

All too often people pit "real life" against metaphysics, which they imagine has gotten lost in some castle in the clouds that it dreamt up for itself. But in fact, whenever life and death are truly on the line, it is in fact very hard for us *not* to do metaphysics.

27. Mortality and Natality

Earlier we saw a definition of man as an animal who does metaphysics, and who cannot help but do metaphysics. But we did not go far enough. To this it should be added that he *exists* in a metaphysical way. Anthropology itself—in the sense of our humanity, what it means to be human—implies a metaphysical appeal.[1] Human existence is ontological from the start. Heidegger brought this to the fore in the new name that he gave the human being: the *Dasein*. In standard German *Dasein* just means existence, the fact of "being here." With this as his new name, man no longer appeared as *a being*, the sort of thing that one could identify by this or that characteristic. Henceforth, man was to be seen as a *mode* or *way of being.*

Man cannot be strictly defined by what might be described in an anthropological theory, since an anthropology can only be about a *being*, not a *mode* of being. For that, one needs an ontology. This is why Heidegger saw his own project as an attack on man, writing,

1 See C. Godin, *La Fin de l'homme, op. cit.*, pp. 121 and 209.

with a bit of untranslatable German wordplay, that "[t]he philosophical concept (*Begriff*) is an attack (*Angriff*) on man [...]. The aggressor is not man [...]. Rather, it is the *Da-sein* in man that launches the attack against man, in the act of philosophizing." Later he explains that the project of making the Heideggerian notion of "affective tonality" (*Stimmung*) is so important as to be man's specific difference—and this, recall, at the expense of reason—and will also necessitate "a total transformation of our notion of man (*eine völlige Umstellung unserer Auffassung vom Menschen*)."[2] *Stimmung* is *Befindlichkeit*, the fact of finding oneself, as in "I found myself being in such-and-such a place or such-and-such a condition, or doing such-and-such a thing." Reason observes *what is*, forgetting the subject in so doing—for he "loses himself" or "is lost" in contemplation. But *Stimmung* obliges us to go back and consider the subject as one who finds himself somewhere—namely, in the world. What is more, he finds himself "being here" only precariously, for he is destined to leave it again at death.

Hannah Arendt responded to various philosophies of the mortality of the *Dasein*, especially that of Heidegger, her own teacher, by introducing a complementary notion that she called natality. She took it up from time to time throughout her works, but to my knowledge she never really developed it thoroughly. If the word is of her own invention the idea nonetheless came from her reflection on the thought of an essentially Christian metaphysician, St. Augustine, on whom she had written her doctoral dissertation as a young philosopher. Thereafter she often returned to one of Augustine's lines on the creation of Adam: "It was therefore in order that there might be such a beginning, that a man was created; and before him there was no one (*hoc ergo [sc. initium] ut esset, creatus est homo, ante quem nullus fuit*)."[3] In Arendt's reading, Augustine was breaking with the Homeric way of considering humans as mortals (*brotoi*) by

2   M. Heidegger, *Die Grundbegriffe der Metaphysik. Welt-Endlichkeit-Einsamkeit*, ed. F.-W. von Herrmann. *GA*, 29/30, pp. 31 and 93; see also *Vom Wesen der menschlichen Freiheit. Einleitung in die Philosophie*, ed. H. Tietjen. *GA*, 31, p. 127.
3   Augustine, *De civitate Dei, op. cit.*, XII, 21, t. I, p. 832.

treating them, as it were, as "natals."[4] This is a misreading of Augustine, but that is not important for our purposes. Birth, writes Arendt, is "the miracle that saves the world [...] from its normal, 'natural' ruin." And as such it is divine.[5] Nowadays everyone sings the praises of human creativity, and rightly so. But it is natality that is actually the very foundation of our creativity. It is the first condition of human action. We humans, of course, can and must do things and make things, but this is only because we started out by being born. Man can *make* something new, can *do* something new, because he *is* something new. Whatever this new creature would do would thus itself also be new.

28. The Right to Procreate

All well and good. But how can we really take Adam's case as universally applicable to every human birth? Strictly speaking, if we were to apply it to parenting we would have to arrogate to ourselves qualities that are proper only to God—not just his omnipotence, but also, and above all else, his absolute benevolence. For the God of Genesis can create Adam in the way he does because he also has the power to create Earth as a perfect garden of delight (*gan 'eden*), and then the power to make somebody and put him in it. Christians go further and move from Eden to Paradise, holding that God creates man with the aim of giving him the Absolute Good that he is himself, by uniting man to his own eternal life. But what human parents, even if they are the very best parents imaginable, could possibly offer their children such conditions? And if we cannot, then do we have a right to procreate at all?

The geographer Alexander von Humboldt was said to have held very radical views on this subject. He himself was a lifelong bachelor, probably due to homosexual tendencies, and consequently never had any children. But his justification for bachelorhood was supposedly advanced along atheistic and nihilistic lines, and went as follows:

4   H. Arendt, *The Life of the Mind*, t. II, "Willing." London, Secker & Warburg, 1978, pp. 100–101, 212, and 217.
5   H. Arendt, *The Human Condition* (1958). Chicago, The University of Chicago Press, 1998, p. 247.

"[I consider] marriage a sin, and the procreation of children a crime [...]. I am likewise convinced that anyone who submits to the yoke of marriage is a fool, even a sinner [...]. He is a sinner because by begetting children he gives them life without being able to guarantee their happiness."[6] It is more or less certain that this text is in fact a forgery, but the ideas attributed to Humboldt were definitely in the air at the time when the alleged *Memoirs* were forged (which was when Schopenhauer was at the height of his influence), even if they were not yet so current when Humboldt actually lived. A few years prior to the *Memoirs'* publication, Flaubert, upon learning that his mistress was menstruating again, wrote, "May I pass on to no one the pains and indignities of existence!"[7] Until recently it was only a few isolated individuals like these who would refuse to leave behind any progeny, and it was easy to treat them as old cranks or free-spirited egoists. Today, however, more and more people call for a rejection of procreation, and they are always coming up with new arguments. More important is the fact that this rejection—even when no articulate argument is being made for it—already corresponds to the very concrete behavior of broad swathes of the global population, especially in Europe.

The fact is easy to lament. But the problem remains as posed. We certainly have the most sacred duty to assure the best possible starting conditions for our children, and to make their stay in this world as agreeable as possible. We have, after all, called them into being without asking their permission beforehand.[8] But no one will ever be able to guarantee with absolute certainty that his or her children will be happy.

6   This fragment is found in the *Memoiren Alexander von Humboldt's*, Leipzig, Schäfer, 1861, t. I, pp. 365–366, which cite as a source the journal of a "countess of B," *née* Mlle. de R. (d. 1852). There she is said to recount a conversation that one of her friends supposedly had with Humboldt in Paris in 1812. The text is a forgery; see Kurt R. Biermann, *Miscellanea Humboldtiana*. Berlin, Akademie Verlag, 1990, p. 262.

7   "Que je ne transmettre à personne l'embêtement et les ignominies de l'existence !" G. Flaubert, Letter to Louise Colet, 11 December 1852, *Correspondance, op. cit.*, t. II, p. 205.

8   E. Kant, *Metaphysik der Sitten*, I, "Metaphysische Anfangsgründe der Rechtslehre," I, 2, 3, 2, §28, *WW*, t. IV, p. 394.

To my great shame, I was not aware of David Benatar's 2006 book *Better Never to Have Been* when I was giving the lectures that formed the basis for this book, nor even when I was beginning to revise it for the present edition. There Benatar argues that we not only do not have any duty to procreate, but that in fact we have the duty *not* to do so. We are morally obligated, he says, to put an end to the human adventure. This voluntary extinction of human life would actually be to the advantage (which he conceives as pleasure, in a utilitarian sense of the term) of those who might otherwise be born.[9] It would be all too easy to dismiss this thesis as merely another effort to shock and scandalize the bourgeoisie by advancing the most blatant paradox thinkable. I see it instead as the result of intellectual honesty in trying to draw, with all frankness and clarity, the ultimate conclusions of the immanent logic of atheism, which I, too, am attempting to formulate here, albeit in broad strokes and from the outside. Atheism, following this line of reasoning, admits that it has no argument in favor of the existence of man. In this case, it would seem that the name that atheism has appropriated for itself since the Victorian era, *humanism*, has assumed a rather ironic tone.

Be that as it may. The challenge stands. How should we respond to it? Nietzsche thought he had an answer for the first exponent of pessimism, Schopenhauer, with whose thought he was constantly engaging throughout the whole of his corpus. Against the ascetic renunciation that Schopenhauer preached, Nietzsche proposed a Dionysiac embrace of life, with all its tragic dimensions.[10] He took as a kind of watchword the "love of fate", *amor fati*, an expression with a certain Stoic allure to it.[11] But in Nietzsche's answer the only question that really matters here went unaddressed. It might work out for me all right if I love fate with respect to the lot that I find ready-made for me as soon as I arrive on the scene. And with the "eternal return of the same," I also have no need to leave my singularity behind. In fact, the opposite is true: I am bound all the

9   D. Benatar, *Better Never to Have Been. The Harm of Coming into Existence*. Oxford, Oxford University Press, 2006. David Benatar teaches at the University of Cape Town in South Africa. I owe my awareness of this book to M. Vincent Aubin (Lyon).
10   F. Nietzsche, Fragment 16 (32), Spring–Summer 1888, *KSA*, t. XIII, p. 492.
11   F. Nietzsche, *Die fröhliche Wissenschaft*, IV, §276, *KSA*, t. III, p. 521.

more decisively to it. But do we have to submit to being a destiny, a fate, *for others*? Again, it might be a very good thing to accept bravely the existence that I have received. Perhaps I may even find a kind of heroic joy in this acceptance. But do I have the right to impose such an existence *on others*?

29. The End of Contingency

We are, after all, the ones who impose existence on others. It is less and less possible to be deluded about our responsibility by blaming impersonal forces like instinct. In his day, Schopenhauer could still attribute the human choices for sexual partners and for children to the will to live, which he took to be blind, but nonetheless capable of deceiving us.[12] This is hardly plausible anymore as an account of the choice to procreate, in the age of cheap chemical or mechanical contraception, at least in many parts of the world.

The American philosopher Richard Rorty, who passed away in 2005, once described the perfect society—that is, one totally stripped of any trace of divinity—as follows:

> [I]n its ideal form, the culture of liberalism would be one which was enlightened, secular, through and through. It would be one in which no trace of divinity remained, either in the form of a divinized world or a divinized self. Such a culture would have no room for the notion that there are non-human forces to which human beings should be responsible. It would drop, or drastically reinterpret, not only the idea of holiness but those of "devotion to truth" and of "fulfillment of the deepest needs of the spirit." The process of de-divinization [...] would, ideally, culminate in our no longer being able to see any use for the notion that finite, mortal, contingently existing human beings might derive the meanings of their

12 A. Schopenhauer, *Die Welt als Wille und Vorstellung*, *op. cit.*, t. II, II, 4, Ch. XLIV, p. 684. Schopenhauer was not ignorant of the existence of the means of contraception, which are in fact very ancient; see t. I, IV, §69, p. 543.

lives from anything except other finite, mortal, contingently existing human beings.[13]

It is a striking passage. It would be hard to describe with more talent or eloquence than Rorty here deploys a situation that, very simply, *is not* the case and will be even less so in the future, and furthermore to put it forward as an ideal state of affairs. Let us take a look at the three adjectives that Rorty uses to characterize human beings. Our existence is indeed "finite" and "mortal", and we scarcely need to explain the fact at length. But "contingent"? Now here we have something begging for a distinction. If we take the adjective in a strict sense—namely, as describing something that is capable of not being—then we can easily admit its use here. Each of us is just what he is through the fortuitous encounter of two individuals who themselves came about in the same way, and so on. But if we take contingency as the notion that our existence is the product of strictly accidental chance, then precisely the opposite is true: our existence is less and less contingent. In our Western or Westernizing societies, this existence is increasingly the result of freely, consciously, and indeed carefully planned decisions. It is, for example, extremely interesting that nowadays an expression like "family planning" no longer raises eyebrows and has in fact become as common as can be—despite the fact that it is hardly a self-evident concept.

Moreover, advances in applied biology have left not only the generation of embryos and fetuses, or the interruption of their development, to human choice. Their characteristics, too, may be chosen, as science fiction authors have long foreseen.

30. Producing Humans

The first was probably Aldous Huxley in his *Brave New World* (1932), which has since become universally famous and almost proverbial. In the titular new world, human matter is cultivated and grown in gigantic incubators where it receives the distinguishing characteristics that will

13   R. Rorty, "The Contingency of a Liberal Community," in *Contingency, Irony and Solidarity*. Cambridge, Cambridge University Press, 1989, p. 45.

predestine it to belong to one caste or another. Huxley's novelistic imagination was ignited by very real and quite openly acknowledged projects that professional biologists were already starting to undertake. From 1923 onward, for example, the Scotsman J.B.S. Haldane had been working on the possibilities for what he called "ectogenesis," i.e. the *in vitro* production of human beings.[14]

Today, as but one example of the selection for or against certain characteristics in human progeny, ultrasonic echography allows us to find out the fetus' sex quite early on in a pregnancy. In some countries it is used to eliminate girls, whom the parents cannot marry off without a costly dowry, and so to favor boys who will pass on the family name. Plenty of haunting stories about this kind of sex selection have surfaced, especially in the East. Some women have as many abortions as necessary until they find they are carrying a fetus of the desired sex, which is to say male. The disequilibrium between the numbers of girls and boys has already reached noticeable proportions.

We do not need to go any further into these sci-fi nightmares, and even less into their real-life counterparts. But in any case, the fact stands: the very existence of human beings depends more and more on the free will of human beings.

There are various causes for the drop in birth rates in Western countries, but the role played by socio-economic circumstances—be these positive or negative, structural or short-term—is important. Among the oft-cited causes I will cite a few, and in no particular order: the lengthening duration of studies, women's employment, the difficulties young people face in trying to find stable jobs and housing, etc.

The question of such "causes" (supposing that the experts would accept this term) will not preoccupy me here, if only because I am not a particularly competent judge in these matters. I therefore take no position on any of them. In particular, I am not claiming that the demographic decline in developed countries is due to "metaphysical" causes—for example, to the decline of religious faith. If I may make a rather elementary

---

14 J.B.S. Haldane, *Daedalus or Science and the Future. A Paper Read to the Heretics, Cambridge on February 4th, 1923*. London, Kegan Paul *et al.*, 1924, pp. 46–48, and see also p. 92.

distinction, I am not interested in *causes* but in *reasons*. More precisely, not in the *past* causes of the *present* situation, but in the reasons that we must have *now* to determine what the *future* will be like.

The predictions of the biologists and the novelists, if predictions they are, should permit us to pursue our thought experiment at last. Let us imagine, then, that the next generation will be neither conceived by nor born of human beings, but produced by some enormous machine and then raised by various social institutions with the requisite competencies. (True, such a system might have certain disadvantages or raise certain moral objections, of which I will say nothing here; but it would at least resolve some or all of the socio-economic difficulties I have just described, as well as the basic, biologically driven inequality between the sexes: the male inseminating and the female bearing the fetus, nursing the infant, taking on most of the child-rearing, etc.) To produce the desired quantity of humans, and at the right moment, with all other conditions in place the only thing that the present generation would have to do would be to push a button.

It may sound outlandish. But as far as the question of the legitimacy of our own practices is concerned, we have not really taken even a single step beyond our current situation. For, ultimately, would anything oblige us to push the button? Would it even be morally acceptable to do so?

CHAPTER IX
Beneath Good and Evil

Before we try to answer these questions, let us step back and take a broad look at the last few centuries of modernity. It was during this period that the modern project, launched in the seventeenth century, was finally able to bring about the technical conditions needed for its realization.

31. The Age of Being

Without taking the schema too seriously, we might characterize the history of the nineteenth, twentieth, and perhaps the twenty-first centuries in terms of the transcendentals we saw earlier. On this very crude account, we could have some fun by saying that the transcendentals have appeared one after another at the crux of the most intense problems that have come up over the centuries. The nineteenth was dominated by the problem of the *Good*, the twentieth by that of *Truth*. Will the twenty-first belong to *Being*?

Let us take each of these in turn. The chief question in the nineteenth century was social in nature. It was raised in Europe and in the regions of the world where Europe had launched its various colonial adventures. For in Europe and in the overseas extensions of the European cultural sphere—such as the United States—a capitalist economy unchecked by legislation created social structures whose injustices were plain to see, and in so doing produced a class that found itself excluded from meaningful participation in society.

The social question in the West, then, concerned the need for justice for those hurt by competition and sought ways in which the excluded class might be reintegrated into society. The evil of the day consisted in exploitation, poverty, and exclusion. In the colonies, meanwhile, the question arose in the context of the power differential between the colonizers and their colonized subjects.

In the twentieth century, a new transcendental arrived on the scene to join the Good: Truth. It was accompanied by its contrary, falsehood or deceit.[1]

The dominant issue then was the emergence of ideological regimes, by which I mean Leninism and Nazism. They were both made possible by the new paradigmatic form that truth had assumed by their day—namely, scientific truth. This is not about the truths of the sciences, which are always partial and tentative, but instead about the "Truth" of "Science", as imagined by those who have no practical experience of it. Ideology, in short, is impossible without the scientism that marked the end of the nineteenth century.

These two ideologies each claimed an incontestable truth. Nazism presented itself as a sober worldview based on scientific biology; Leninism presented itself as one based on scientific economics and on the new science of societal evolution that Marx thought he had founded.

The long war against ideology—both in its Nazi version and even more clearly in its Leninist version, which is the most perfect form of ideology—was not primarily waged on the plane of good and evil. It can only be understood as a struggle between the true and the false, or more exactly between the truthful and the deceitful. The chief protest made against socialism was not of a moral nature. Instead, it consisted in showing that the claim that there was such a thing as "really existing Socialism" (*real existierender Sozialismus*) somewhere out there was a lie, pure and simple, and that this socialism, however perfect it might be, nonetheless had the slight flaw of not really existing. As Aleksandr Solzhenitsyn put it, the worst suffering that the ideological regime caused—worse even than all the poverty and the oppression, in spite of the fact that these were indeed quite real—was that it forced those who were subjected to it to lie. Similarly, in his view, the first step in liberating yourself from this suffering was simply refusing to make yourself complicit in the lie.[2]

---

1   I draw my inspiration here from the thought of Alain Besançon, especially from his reflection on the notion of ideology.

2   A. Solzhenitsyn, *Lettre aux dirigeants de l'Union soviétique* (*A Letter to the Soviet Leaders*). Paris, Seuil, 1974, p. 36.

So much for the last two centuries and their transcendentals. I would tentatively wager that the twenty-first will be dominated by the question of Being.

Of course, the concern for the good and the duty to speak the truth are very far from obsolete. They will be around as long as evil and false-hood remain in the world and thus perhaps up until the very last day. But our socio-economic issues, while they have not been entirely re-solved, have at least calmed somewhat, at least in the West. And the ide-ological temptation, though it has not disappeared, nonetheless no longer has the support that it once enjoyed from massively armed states.

The current age, however, has added Being as a further dimension to these old problems. And Being is hardly just another level built atop the edifice of the other transcendentals. Rather, it lies beneath them: it is their very foundation.

32. The Infra-Moral Basis of Morality

Let us first hear an objection. It comes from Emmanuel Levinas, who, playing on a rather overused line, once famously asked, "To be or not to be, *is* that the question?"[3] With this Levinas meant to respond to Hei-degger, who had tried to bring Plato's and Aristotle's questioning of Being back into philosophical fashion and thereby to rescue it from the oblivion into which it had supposedly slipped. For Levinas, over and above the consideration of ontology as a question of Being there is an ethical appeal, the unconditional claim of the Good. But it may yet be that it was Hamlet who had the question right after all—as I will try to show.

Another line from Levinas can serve as our point of departure. As he saw it, "birth, which is unchosen, and indeed is impossible to choose, [is] the great drama of contemporary thought."[4] On the one hand, this means that birth is difficult to accept. Indeed, birth is an absolute

3   E. Levinas, *Éthique comme philosophie première*, 6, ed. J. Rolland. Paris, Rivages poche, 1998, p. 107.
4   E. Levinas, *Totalité et infinie. Essai sur l'extériorité*. The Hague, Nijhoff, 1961, p. 199.

refutation of all human claims to self-affirmation and to autonomy as the creation of the self by the self. But we should also take this *drama* in the literal sense of the Greek word, as a deed or act of a certain pre-eminence, and see birth as the action that makes every other action possible. Hannah Arendt's reflections offer a powerful echo of this idea, as we just saw.[5]

There is a paradox concerning birth that we should note. A successful act of reproduction is the first condition of every human life, and the existence of human beings is the first condition—a necessary one, albeit not sufficient—for the decision that these human beings may eventually make to lead a fully human life, in the richest possible sense, by giving it a moral dimension. But this first condition of the moral life, the existence of human beings, is one that is itself beyond the scope of morality. Morality is essentially concerned with relations between existing human beings. Consider also the notions of "your duties to yourself," "what you owe yourself," as we sometimes say (or used to say, the expressions being a bit worn by now). Or again, there is the question of human obligations toward animals, which has been in the public eye for several decades now. Obviously none of this has any meaning if there are no people who exist as moral, rights-bearing subjects. And even if we reject the idea of animal "rights", the more easily defensible notion that we humans at least have responsibilities toward them also presupposes the coexistence, and therefore the *existence*, of various species, including our own.

Still, on the basis of the precondition that we exist we have no reason to suppose that we have a duty to bring children into the world. We can admire and praise people who do a good job taking care of the children they already have, in the ways they provide for them, raise them, etc. But this does not mean we can say that it would be good *in itself* to want to have children, or inversely that it would be evil *in itself* to want to have none at all. After all, *to whom* would we owe this duty? Hans Jonas, for one, grounded the idea of an obligation to keep the human adventure going in our responsibility toward the "*idea* of man", from which he derived an "ontological imperative". He rightly noted that "the first principle of an 'ethics of futurity' (*Zukünftigkeitsethik*)

5   See above, §27, pp. 63–65.

is not to be sought in ethics as a theory of action, but rather in metaphysics."[6]

Dieter Birnbacher, meanwhile, asks:

> Why should the duty to have children need to be owed to anyone at all? It could instead play a valuable role as a prototype for any obligation that can't be said to be *owed* to anyone or to exist *with respect to* anyone. If this duty exists as a moral duty, then it is a duty without relation to anything, of any kind at all, that we encounter.[7]

This is nicely put. But Birnbacher's use of the word "prototype" obscures the fact that he has posited an obligation of this kind—of which, in fact, procreation would end up being the only instance—entirely *ad hoc*, and in a way that gives the term a decidedly Pickwickian shade.

The question stands, then. I may do my children wrong, if I do decide to have any, by raising them poorly or mistreating them. But whom am I wronging when I opt not to have any children at all? Certainly not those whom I never end up calling into existence.

One might perhaps argue that I am doing wrong to other, already existing adults, for example, because I am leaving them the burden of begetting and rearing the next generation, which in time will come to care for me when I am no longer able to work. There is some truth in this, but the reproach could be turned against itself. If I have had children, what right did I have to bring them into the world to provide for my needs? Have we not heard it said often enough by now that we must always treat human beings as ends, and never just as means? And if we justify procreation in terms of our retirement plans, would we not simply be instrumentalizing our neighbors to the highest degree?

Various ancient philosophers considered the question of whether marriage and procreation were justifiable, and not all of them came down entirely positively on the two points. Those in favor included Epicurus, Zeno, Cicero,

---

6   H. Jonas, *Das Prinzip Verantwortung, op. cit.*, pp. 91–92. Original emphasis. See also p. 185.

7   D. Birnbacher, *Verantwortung für zukünftige Generationen, op. cit.*, p. 133.

and the Peripatetics whose ethical teachings were collected by Stobaeus.[8] Those opposed included the Cynics and Democritus, who supposedly defended his stance with the following observation: "Having children involves many a grave danger, not a few pains, and scant pleasures—and these last are meager and faint."[9] This line was issued from the point of view of a potential father concerned, of course, with his own comfort and pleasure.

Marriage and procreation have always seemed so obvious to so many that arguments for them have only rarely been formulated. For the ancients, at least, this was a question that occurred to none but philosophers, and thus to an extremely small minority of people, albeit one that saw itself as an important elite. It was hardly an issue for the rest of humanity, which followed its instincts in this regard. For those of us living today, on the other hand, it *is* an issue, largely due to a very convenient technical possibility and a massive social fact, one that is practiced on a very large scale, defended by the dominant cultural discourse, and supported by decisions made at the highest levels of government: contraception.

For humanity to continue to exist, we humans must act, implicitly or explicitly, in accordance with the idea that life *itself* is a good thing. And it must be good not merely for those of us who are to pass it on, but just as much for the eventual children who will have to receive it from us if we choose to do so.

To be quite clear, it certainly is not necessary for everyone to be explicitly aware of this. It is enough for the cultural atmosphere to be conducive to the idea, as it was in ancient times, when people took their bearings from the experience of a world that was eternal both in its existence and in its order. In those days humanity understood itself, too, as part of this natural order, in which species were fixed and permanent. The ideal was to steadily replace the dead with newcomers, such that the human race might attain at least the semblance of a constant headcount from generation to generation.

---

8   Diogenes Laërtius, *Vies, doctrines et sentences des hommes illustres*, X, 119 (Epicurus); VII, 121 (Zeno); Cicero, *De finibus*, III, 20, 68, ed. T. Schiche. Stuttgart, Teubner, 1961, p. 116; Stobaeus, *Anthology*, II, 94, 13–15.

9   Stobaeus, *Anthology*, IV, 24, 29, 31–33; 26, 25–26 (DK 68 B 275–280).

One might well ask whether the present age, at least in Europe, does not promote the exact opposite idea. John Paul II could scarcely have put it any better when he spoke of a "culture of death."[10] To be sure, the expression is absurd in itself, a contradiction in terms. Culture, as such, must be a culture of life. Only a "non-culture" could be based on death. But, precisely as an oxymoron, it manages to capture the intrinsically paradoxical nature of our present situation.

33. The Sterility of Atheism

Perhaps nobody has expressed the problem facing us today better than an author who wrote long ago in an age when the last preconditions for the birth of our own civilization were just falling into place: Rousseau. The text I shall cite comes from a famous passage in *Émile*, the "Profession of Faith of the Savoyard Curate," where Rousseau sets down his own views on religion. The excerpt below comes from lines that he relegated to an obscure footnote, but which to me seem to be extremely important for us today:

> If atheism does not lead to bloodshed, it is less out of love for peace than through indifference to the good. For whatever should happen [i.e. in the world], it matters little to the supposed sage, so long as he may remain in the quiet of his study. *His principles do not kill anyone, but they do prevent men from being born*—by destroying the mores by which they would multiply, by distancing them from their own species, by reducing all their affections to a secret egoism as deadly to the population as it is to virtue. The philosopher's indifference is like the tranquility of the State under the yoke of despotism. It is the tranquility of death; it is more destructive than war itself.[11]

10 John Paul II, *Evangelium Vitae*, 1995, I, §12; the expression is also in C. Godin, *La Fin de l'homme, op. cit.*, p. 219.
11 J.-J. Rousseau, *Émile*, IV, *Œuvres complètes, op. cit.*, t. IV, pp. 632–633. My emphasis.

Following Rousseau, then, I should like to address a question or two to our nihilists, whether their brand of nihilism be grim or cheerful. So, then, nihilists: Your principles, assuming they should hold general sway, would have as an eminently positive consequence—and let us tentatively admit this even if experience proves otherwise—an end to all wars of religion, or better yet, an end to all wars waged for the sake of, or on the pretext of, any ideas whatsoever, be they religious or not. No one would slit his neighbor's throat for your principles. People would quite literally want to die "for nothing," since what they would believe in would be precisely this "nothing".

But would your convictions also allow us to live? By this I mean: *even if nihilism will not kill us, can it bring us life?* I do not mean to raise the question of "reasons for living", for, as you will rightly object, why do we need any such reasons? They are hardly indispensable. I grant you that. Once we are alive, there is no need at all for any *reason* to stay that way. A little inertia is enough, and inertia need not prevent us from filling our days with any number of interesting activities, hopefully even some admirable ones.

On the other hand, we absolutely *do* need reasons to *give* life. A principled, consistent, and nihilistic atheist who had children would be, according to his own principles, morally reprehensible, as we saw already in the Pseudo-Humboldt.[12] But we can find this outlook again much closer to our own day, in Emil Cioran, for example. Looking back on his life, he congratulated himself for having at least avoided committing the grave crime of having children:

> The only thing I am proud of having understood very early on, before my twentieth year, is that one must not have children. My horror at marriage, family, and all social conventions derives from this recognition. It is a crime to transmit one's own flaws to any offspring, and so to force them to suffer the same trials you have undergone, atop some Calvary that could end up being even worse than your own. I have never been able to consent to giving life to someone who

12   See above, §28, pp. 65–68.

would thereby inherit my own misfortunes and miseries. Parents are all irresponsible, even murderous. It is mercy that forbids a man to become a parent, a father, a *"begetter"*—the most awful word I know.[13]

34. The Abusive Bus

In January 2009, British atheists launched a publicity campaign sponsored by, among others, the English scientist Richard Dawkins. In London and other cities of the United Kingdom, public buses bore placards with the following message: "There's probably no God. Now stop worrying and enjoy your life."[14] God seems to show up here as someone whose existence is grounds for our anxiety, someone who might keep us from enjoying life. This strikes me as a bit of a caricature even if it is the behavior of some believers, in times past and still today, that is in part responsible for this rather dour picture of God. But I will insist here neither on the readiness with which so many atheists succumb to the temptation to go after a straw man (or straw god, as the case may be), nor on the possible causes of this intellectual poverty.

What I would prefer to do is to turn to the use of the possessive pronoun in the phrase "enjoy *your* life." It is not strictly necessary. They could just as easily have written "enjoy life." But its presence is telling, almost a Freudian slip. The phrase expresses quite consistently, if probably unconsciously, the logic of nihilistic atheism. If God does not exist then the living have the right to enjoy *their own* lives, the particular lives that belong to them each individually. But they could never force anyone else to enjoy life without committing an awful crime.

If this sort of atheism were to become universal, and then follow its own internal logic all the way through to its ultimate practical

13 E.M. Cioran, *Cahiers. 1957–1972*, Note between November 11 and 12, 1962. Paris, Gallimard, 1997, p. 125.
14 I commented at greater length on this slogan during a colloquium organized by the Lumen Christi Institute (Chicago), *Secularism*, 25–26 June, 2010., Paris, Collège des Bernardins.

conclusion, it would be perfectly deserving of the other name that it is known by, at least in the Anglo-Saxon world: secularism. There are revealing cognates in French, which has two adjectives derived from the same Latin word, *saeculum*: *séculier*, literally meaning "of this world," and *séculaire*, literally meaning "of a century." Both these senses come together in secularism, for the project of an atheistic humanity may perhaps enjoy *its* life, but that life may not last much longer than a century.

It could well be that the whole process of evolution that gave rise to life, and subsequently to the existence of the human species, is the product of blind chance. But even if that is so, it is up to us to decide whether to continue this story or to put an end to it. Even though we ourselves did not come into the world freely, we *are* free to call others into it.

This, though, we only have the right to do if we can really say that life is also something good for those whom we bring here. And for this to be the case it is not enough for life to be merely more or less *pleasant*. Few people deny that it is. I do not, at any rate. But life, our mode of *being*, must also, and as such, be *good*. And this must be true no matter what trials and tribulations life will bring to the people who will not have asked to come here—for no matter how we might limit their difficulties and ease what suffering they endure, as it is our duty to do, there is no way we can be sure of sparing the newcomers from all harm.

For this reason we must affirm—whether in accordance with appearances or in spite of them—that Being and Goodness coincide. And here we have little use for a "weak" good. We need instead the strongest of all goods, the Good writ large.

CHAPTER X
Metaphysics as the Object of Freedom

This situation may force us to reopen an old debate that to all appearances had been settled long ago and even forgotten as a live issue. The conceptual move needed here is a modern version of what in ancient philosophy would amount to a shift from Aristotle back to his teacher, Plato.

35. Back to Plato

Aristotle came to criticize the Platonic Idea of the Good, or at least to exclude it from the scope of his ethics, which he instead limited to the study of the Good insofar as it could be realized by man: the "practical" or "practicable good" (*prakton agathon*).[1]

Plato, for his part, explained the Idea of the Good by means of a famous metaphor involving the sun. In its emphasis on illumination, this image has inspired so much philosophical reflection over the years that some have even spoken of a "metaphysics of light."[2] But Plato also made use of another aspect of the metaphor, one he presented much more succinctly, yet only in passing, which perhaps explains why it has not been investigated much. The sun, he noted, allows visible things to be seen by virtue of its illumination. But it also enables them to come into being, or undergo "becoming" (*genesis*), to enjoy growth (*auxē*), and to find nourishment (*trophē*).[3] He did not have to insist on this, for he was

1 Aristotle, *Nicomachean Ethics*, I, 7, 1097a23.
2 See for example W. Beierwaltes, *Lux intelligibilis. Untersuchung zur Licht-metaphysik der Griechen*, Diss. München 1952 (unpublished); the expression "metaphysics of light" probably comes from C. Bäumker.
3 Plato, *Republic*, VI, 509b2–4.

merely stating the obvious, i.e. that the sun is important for all kinds of biological development. Later his disciple Aristotle was to give a more thorough account of the nature of generation or "coming-to-be" in a whole treatise on the subject, where it is situated within a whole cosmography.[4] Aristotle would even subtly suggest that all *human procreation* presupposes the presence of the sun in the background: "Man, and the sun with him, begets man" (*anthrōpos anthrōpon genna kai hēlios*).[5]

Let us dwell for a moment on Plato's initial observation. The sun makes plants grow, makes them sprout up out of the ground. In so doing they become visible. But more essentially, they thereby become capable of nourishing themselves on the sun's rays. It is similar with the Good, which not only illuminates what is already present, but is also what brings forth things that are knowable and enables them to orient themselves toward it. The Idea of the Good, Plato famously went on to say, is beyond Being (*epekeina tēs ousias*).[6] Centuries after Plato's death, this phrase was to become the object of the Neo-Platonists' constant meditation. In our time it was adopted and popularized by Levinas, who used it as the subtitle of one of his major works.[7] As for what it originally meant, the Platonic Good may be formally defined as that on account of which Being (*einai*) and the fact that a thing is what it is (*ousia*) happen to come to (*proseinai*) anything that is known.[8]

I would like to pursue Plato's insights by looking at something that the later tradition would add to his thought. The idea is this. Things that are known receive Being in various ways, each according to its own

---

4   Aristotle, *On Generation and Corruption*, II, 10, the whole chapter, and especially 336b17–18.
5   Aristotle, *Physics*, II, 2, 194b13.
6   Plato, *Republic,* VI, 509b9.
7   E. Levinas, *Autrement qu'être ou Au-delà de l'essence*. The Hague, Nijhoff, 1974.
8   Plato, *Republic*, VI, 509b7–8. It could be that the *kai* only serves the epexegetical function of making the verb "to be" or "being" explicit, in which case after "being" (*einai*) we would have to translate "namely, what they are." The *proseinai*, literally "to be added to" or "to come as an addition to" something, is perhaps the origin of Avicenna's ontology; see above, §12, p. 30–31.

nature. Rocks and the like do not receive it in the same way as plants do, nor plants as animals, nor other animals as humans. Each kind of thing receives what it needs in order for it to attain its own good: "To each according to his needs," we might say. For rocks, the good consists in merely existing, and so in a sense it simply coincides with Being. For living things, the good consists in surviving individually as well as in reproducing as a species; it also consists in being, but living things, unlike rocks, must seek it out. As for us human beings, it is in our unique character as *free* beings that we are left with the task of seeking the Good, and this allows us to be most fully what we are. Freedom, we might say, is the means by which we access the Good.

36. The Emergence of Freedom

This brief reflection has taken us deep into philosophical territory and indeed to its very center, for philosophy is itself an affirmation of our freedom. While that affirmation was already prefigured in ancient times, it has taken until the modern period for it to find its most striking expression.[9] This is because philosophy might be understood as the ultimate development of the capacity for *logos* that defines us as a species.

Indeed, in the traditional definition, man was seen as a living being endowed with *logos*, and in that notion of *logos* the idea of freedom was already present, albeit implicitly. It did come up in Aristotle's theory of "rational potencies" (*dynamis meta logou*): in contrast to irrational potencies, which were each limited to resulting in a single effect, rational potencies could be realized either in an effect or in its contrary.[10] Nonetheless, in philosophy freedom was a concept that most of the time remained implicit. For the ancients, freedom (*eleutheria*) was above all a social reality: the public status of a free man as opposed to that of a slave.[11] Conceptually it surfaced only rarely.

9   See my *Introduction au monde grec*, Chatou, La Transparence, 2005, pp. 10–11.
10 Aristotle, *Metaphysics*, Book IX (Theta) , 2.
11 We find the same situation in Islam in its Classical Age: see F. Rosenthal, *The Muslim Concept of Freedom Prior to the Nineteenth Century*. Leiden, Brill, 1960.

One other example in antiquity, however, came from Alexander of Aphrodisias, who claimed that nothing was more proper to man than the fact that his actions were under his own control (*eph' hēmin*).[12] Some time later, in the Patristic age, St. Gregory of Nyssa wrote:

> He Who created man, in order that man might share in His own virtues, and the One Who, in molding man's nature, placed within it the principle of all that is beautiful, in order that his every capacity might orient his desire toward the Divine Attribute corresponding to it—this Creator, I say, would not have deprived man of the most beautiful and the most precious endowment of all: and here I mean the grace of being independent (*adespotos*) and free (*autexousios*).[13]

In the Middle Ages, a Franciscan named Peter John Olivi gave the idea a powerful image—especially for us today, living in the age of computers—when he claimed that a man without freedom would be nothing but a calculating beast. Dante, too, spoke of free will as the most precious gift that God ever gave man.[14] But it was probably Rousseau who first explicitly substituted liberty for reason as the specific difference of the human race: "It is not [...] so much the understanding that constitutes man's specific distinction from all the other animals, as it is his character as a free agent."[15]

Kant's assertion of the "primacy of practical reason" opened up a whole new field for metaphysics, and into the breach rushed the German Idealists, with Fichte at their head.[16] In the words of the young (and still

---

12 Alexander of Aphrodisias, *De anima liber cum mantissa*, ed. I. Bruns. Berlin, Reimer, 1887, p. 175.

13 Gregory of Nyssa, *Discours catéchétique (Catechetical Oration)*, V, 9–10, ed. L. Méridier. Paris, Picard, 1908, pp. 30–32. English translation by James Herbert Srawley, modified.

14 Dante, *De monarchia*, I, 12, 6, and *Commedia, Paradiso*, V, 19–22.

15 J.-J. Rousseau, *Discours sur l'origine de l'inégalité*, I, *Œuvres complètes*, *op. cit.*, p. 141.

16 E. Kant, *Kritik der praktischen Vernunft*, ed. K. Vorländer. Hamburg, Meiner, 1929, pp. 138–140.

Fichtean) Schelling: "The Alpha and Omega of all philosophy is freedom."[17]

This philosophical revolution was in step with the very concrete historical development of modernity, which, in its economic, social, and political aspects, in effect amounted to the progressive realization of freedom. And here it was no longer the freedom of a single person, nor again of an elite: on the horizon, at least, it was the freedom of all people. Hegel saw freedom as the end of the entire motion of history.[18] For my part, I would like to quote a line from the Catholic Anglo-Bavarian historian Lord Acton, who spent much of his life preparing to write a grand "History of Liberty" but never managed to do so: "Liberty is not a means to a higher political end," he said. "It is itself the highest political end."[19] More generally, we could say that freedom is not a means to a higher end of any kind, political or not. It is an end in itself.

37. Freedom and the Good

For us humans, as I noted, it is through our freedom that we have access to the Good. We attain it through our deeds (*praxis*). The Good, for us, is what we do, or rather what we should do.

As far as our deeds are concerned, the Aristotelian good is, well, good enough. In this sense Aristotle was certainly right to bracket aside the Idea of the Good when he was discussing ethics and looking for certain rules for how to act. To put it in a modern, Kantian key, he wanted to answer the question, "What should I do?" And to answer this kind of question we might well limit ourselves to a search for the "practical good", the good that we can actually do.[20] Conceiving of the Good in this way, however, will prove to be insufficient if it is not moral actions

---

17 F. Schelling, letter to Hegel, 4 February 1795, *Briefe an und von Hegel*, ed. J. Hoffmeister, Hamburg, Meiner, 1969, t. I, p. 22.

18 G.W.F. Hegel, *Philosophe der Geschichte*, ed. H. Glockner. Stuttgart, Frommann, 1928, t. XI, Introduction, pp. 44–47.

19 Lord Acton, *The History of Freedom in Antiquity* (1877), "Ancient Rome," in *Selected Writings*, ed. J.R. Fears. Indianapolis, Liberty Press, 1985, t. I, p. 22.

20 See above, §35, p. 82.

that we are trying to produce, but the moral agents *of* those actions, the acting subjects of the moral life who may themselves wonder what it is their moral duty to do.

Aristotle often voiced his objection to Plato's Ideas, saying that they did nothing, withdrawn as they were in the distant splendor of their heavenly realm, where they remained forever inert, inactive, and therefore ineffective and useless.[21] Now, it is certainly true that the Forms are in no way efficient causes. But perhaps we could say that they act like catalysts in chemistry: while they may not "do" anything in that they themselves do not react with the other chemicals in the flask, their mere presence does make the reactions of those other chemicals possible. In this sense, the Forms' presence is what permits the very causality of causes, including efficient ones, to work—which is to say it enables their action precisely *as* causes.

It is likewise true of the Good taken as such and not merely insofar as it is doable. Perhaps its presence is not absolutely indispensable for human beings to act morally, but it *is* indispensable for humanity to continue to exist at all.

At this point it would be all too easy, even tempting, to dream of paddling back somewhere upstream of modernity to a time when individual freedom was guided or else checked by institutions, customs, mores, and so on. Some thinkers—hardly insignificant thinkers, at that—have indeed tried to help us remember just how much of all this we have lost with the passing of time, and insofar as that awareness has not itself passed into oblivion we are indebted to them. I am thinking above all of the Englishman Edmund Burke. His *Reflections on the Revolution in France* (1790), for instance, forcefully reminds us that *liberty* cannot exist without being rooted in *the liberties* of a particular social group.[22]

Nonetheless, even if one were to grant the possibility of turning back the clock, such is really not my aim here. It is in fact quite the opposite. I would like to take modernity at its word and to take it more seriously than it takes

---

21 Aristotle, *Metaphysics*, Z, 8, 1033b28, and see the references cited in Bonitz, *Index aristotelicus*, 599a46–49.
22 E. Burke, *Reflections on the Revolution in France*, ed. J.G.A. Pocock. Indianapolis, Hackett, 1987.

itself—to radicalize it, and to see where it leads. Recall Marx's famous play on words, that to be radical is to grasp things by the root. "For man, however," he said, "the root is man himself."[23] That line is as gratuitous as it is absurd and need not detain us here. The point is that we ought to consider the conditions that make "the liberty of the Moderns," as Benjamin Constant called it in his reflections on the political sphere, possible at all.[24]

So for this we, too, should be radical and dig down to the roots of the modern project, all the way to its necessary conditions. These conditions will likely only appear when it seems the project is just about to be fully realized—which is to say, right about now.

We ought to be very happy, first of all, about the modern expansion of the sphere accessible to human freedom, even if this expansion has opened up previously unthinkable possibilities that we might not always wish to see fully realized. No longer is man free only to acquire new abilities or technologies or ways of life, and in the forms he wants them to take. Man is also free to pronounce a universal, irrevocable judgment upon himself, be it to affirm his existence or else to deny it entirely without any chance of turning back. Is it possible to conceive of any higher form of self-determination than this?

To what extent does this kind of liberty need the strong sense of the Good that I mentioned earlier?[25] Freedom without this Good could still choose to stay true to the conditions necessary for its own existence, which would be the consistent choice to make; and this, in any case, would be less a choice than a continuation of what humans have done up until now. But could it still choose itself? A free being will always choose to be free, and it cannot freely choose *not* to be free without running into a contradiction. But would this being choose *to be* at all?

Schopenhauer, we have seen, disapproved of "violent" suicide.[26] At the same time, he was less severe toward those who allowed themselves

23   K. Marx, *Zur Kritik der Hegelschen Rechtsphilosophie*, Einleitung, *Früh-schriften*, ed. S. Landshut. Stuttgart, Kröner, 2004, 7th ed., p. 283.

24   B. Constant, *De la liberté des Anciens comparée à celle des modernes*, *Écrits politiques*, ed. M. Gauchet. Paris, Gallimard, "Folio Essais," 1997, pp. 591–619.

25   See above, §34, p. 81.

26   See above, §20, p. 48.

to starve to death. In so doing, he thought, they succeeded in negating the will itself and not just one of its manifestations. But Schopenhauer hazarded a bolder speculation. "Perhaps there is no one alive who would not already have put an end to his life if such an end were something purely negative, a sudden cessation of existence. But in fact it is something positive, namely the destruction of the body, and this holds us back [...]."[27] In other words, if we did not have bodies, and thus if our suicide did not have to involve destroying them, we would all very probably choose not to be. Elsewhere Schopenhauer has nothing but derision for any talk of angels, but his claim here seems to involve beings not wholly unlike them.

There is in fact a case that takes us as close as possible to the situation that Schopenhauer imagined—namely, when the body in question belongs not to *me*, but to someone else. Specifically, we are dealing with someone else who "exists" only in a virtual sense, who can only ever become real if I really want him to: the child who has yet to be conceived. Destroying such a non-existent child, too, can therefore only ever be a virtual act. And it is the easiest thing we can do.

38. Sacrifice

I am far from the first to propose that we reflect on the connections between freedom, Being, and the Good. Long before the modern age these connections were considered by the philosopher Sallustius, the otherwise obscure author of a little treatise entitled *On the Gods and the World*. It is a compendium of popular philosophy composed late in the fourth century to serve as a kind of official catechism for the refined paganism that the emperor Julian the Apostate wanted to pit against Christianity. It has a Neo-Platonic hue to it and, unsurprisingly, we find there once again the fundamental claim of that tradition—namely, the superiority of the Good over Being.

Sallustius writes that there is very concrete proof for this claim: "Noble souls despise existence (*to einai*), as compared to the good (*to agathon*),

---

27 A. Schopenhauer, *Paralipomena, op. cit.*, Ch. XIII, "Über den Selbstmord," §158, p. 366. English translation by E.F.J. Payne, modified.

when they spontaneously rush (*thelein*) into danger for their homeland or their friends, or for the sake of virtue."[28] Man's capacity for self-sacrifice, argued Sallustius, shows that he is capable of putting the Good before Being. This kind of sacrifice is entirely different from suicide. Suicide is a destruction of being, and as such it is sought out of a failure to see that being opens onto the Good. Self-sacrifice, on the other hand, comes from understanding that there is a Good that is accessible to us beyond mere existence.

This is a Good that we can *want*. It is, we saw, in and through the will that the Good becomes accessible to us. The relationship to the Good that is formed in our will is one of trust—of *faith*. Perhaps we can apply what we just said about self-sacrifice in general to faith in particular, which is, after all, the "sacrifice of the intellect". Before anyone protests, let us recall that, contrary to the common misreading of it, this expression is a subjective genitive translation of the Pauline saying *logikē latreia* (*Rom* 12:1). The intellect is not the victim, but as it were the priest offering the sacrifice. And the sacrifice that the intellect offers must be a genuine one. It must certainly not allow itself to be corrupted and destroyed by sinking into nonsense. Faith is a relationship with the Good, and it is by a true act of freedom that this Good is attained.

39. Faith or Death

In speaking of faith here, I do not want to rehearse the tired debate about religion's social utility. That dead horse has beaten quite well enough by now, and from both sides—whether to praise religion as a phenomenon indispensable for the healthy functioning of society, or to condemn it and to unmask it as an ideology that serves as a tool of societal manipulation, especially by the authorities who have an interest in perpetuating the order that maintains their authority. The first view found its earliest champion in the sophist Critias, and it has been defended by thinkers all the way up to Émile Durkheim, including, notably, Joseph de Maistre.[29] The

---

28 Sallustius, *Des dieux et du monde*, V, 3, ed. G. Rochefort. Paris, Les Belles Lettres, 1960, p. 9.

29 Critias, *Sisyphus*, No. 88, Frag. B25, in *Die Fragmente der Vorsokratiker*, eds. H. Diels and W. Kranz, t. II. Berlin, Weidmann, 1968, pp. 386–389.

second dates back most memorably to the radical thinkers of the Enlightenment, but it could be found already in ancient times. Those authors favorably disposed toward religion on social grounds typically only consider what they see as its wholly beneficial influence on the behaviors and mores of a people. Their critics never fail to respond by listing all the evils begotten by "fanaticism", from Lucretius' account of the immolation of Iphigenia up to present-day violence.[30] If someone notes that history has never known a society without religion, these critics rightly reply that the past certainly need not predetermine the future and that nothing need stop us from trying such an experiment.

The question that I am raising here—the question of our trusting relationship with the Good, which I am calling faith—is more radical, since it concerns not religion and the functioning of society, but the relationship between religion and the very existence of mankind on Earth. It is not about man as a social animal or as a moral animal, but rather about the human species in all of its rich and varied dimensions, and across the whole scope of its history. It is not about this or that aspect of humanity's peculiar characteristics (social order, morality, etc.), but about the very survival of the species. That being the case, this sort of experiment is all the more risky: if it should fail, there will be no possibility of starting over and trying again.

Initially, Nietzsche had planned for his Zarathustra to pronounce a line which he later chose not to include in the final draft—one wonders why—and which thus never made it out of his notes and into print. The line ran thus: "We are conducting an experiment (*Versuch*) with truth! Perhaps humanity will perish from it! Onward! (*Wohlan!*)"[31]

How reassuring! Did Nietzsche, or Zarathustra, really believe what he was saying, and was he yet willing to take the risk? In respectable company today the word "Providence" tends to elicit a pitying smile, if not a scandal. But might we suspect that Nietzsche, the son of the Lutheran pastor of Röcken, was clinging in spite of himself to the secularized remains of a naïve faith in some kind of Providence guaranteeing

---

30 Lucretius, *De natura rerum*, I, 80–101; see once again the collection put together by J. Salem, *Cinq Variations…*, *op. cit.*, pp. 17–87.

31 F. Nietzsche, Fragment 25 (305), Spring 1884, *KSA*, t. XI, p. 88.

that no matter what we did everything would turn out all right? I do not know. But when I see people in every domain constantly developing and promoting new practices that threaten human life, probably hoping that "everything will turn out all right," I cannot help thinking that many of our contemporaries really do harbor such an illusion. I certainly do not share this way of imagining Providence as a parachute. The Christian notion of Providence strikes me as much richer than this, more nuanced, granting more room to human freedom and to the logical course of human actions, with all their consequences.

Our entire civilization seems ready to indulge in a gigantic bungee jump. But I am not sure that our cord is fastened to anything. And I wonder, with some concern, whether our doomed experiment has not already begun.

Conclusion

I have tried to show that the image so often made of metaphysics—namely, as a pursuit far removed from reality—is itself very far from reality. In the typical caricature metaphysics is depicted as an ethereal, imaginary superstructure wrongly imposed upon the only thing that truly exists: nature, taken in the sense in which the natural sciences are coming to a more and more precise knowledge of our world each day.

Nature (in this sense) can indeed serve as a foundation, but not for metaphysical projects. The only structures that we can safely build on it, so the story goes, are human societies guided by rules designed to permit everyone to flourish. These rules, it is said, require no basis other than the agreement of the members who make up these societies. Similarly, they have no object other than their safety and well-being. Even if it were possible to do so, which it is not, there is no need to seek help from metaphysical dream-castles in the clouds, whether the heavens they are built in be claimed for God or for Plato's Forms.

But both our knowledge of nature and our self-organization into viable and livable societies presuppose something quite obvious—namely, the very existence of our species, the collectivity that is the knowing, striving subject of such knowledge and such efforts at societal organization. Little by little, the *subjective* character of this collectivity has become more pronounced, in pace with the growth of its capacity for intervening in the course of nature and in its own development—in pace, that is, with the growth of concrete spaces for freedom and agency.

The existence of this collectivity, however, is in no way self-evident. With the growth of the human capacity to choose whether to be or not to be, the need for reasons to make the choice for the former will also become more and more urgent.

The need to justify the very existence of mankind compels us in turn to reexamine a considerable number of premises that shape the basic orientation of modern thought. This reconsideration does not mean that we have to turn our backs on the many important and eminently valuable triumphs that we have achieved over the course of our history, and even less that we have to undertake a nostalgic return to some romanticized past. Quite the opposite: the question is how to ensure that man—the subject and object of these benefits—will be able to continue the adventure that has taken him as far as it has. More precisely, the question is how to get him to *want* to continue it.

Modern thought assumes that this desire is self-evident, and that whatever happens humanity's future is somehow secure. It seeks to solve problems that arise from the *co-existence* of human beings, and it does offer a number of solutions that have proved effective. But it evades the preliminary question of the conditions necessary for our *existence*.

As long as this question goes unaddressed, any answers that we give to others can only be provisional. They will—let us hope—allow us humans to ensure our well-being, to feed ourselves, cure our diseases, clothe ourselves, make peace with each other, attain some level of art and culture—and none of this is negligible. But at the end of the day we will still have to ask whether the fact that there even *are* people who can enjoy such goods is itself something good.

Answering a question like this will require a strong metaphysics. To that end, I will content myself with carrying on the tradition that has been observable since the last century, as I discussed at the beginning of this book, of exposing the intrinsically metaphysical dimensions of human life. But here I take human life in a very concrete sense: that of the mere continuation of our species' biological existence. Metaphysics, far from being a superfluous superstructure, turns out to be our indispensable infrastructure, the foundation necessary for the continuation of human life on earth. Preparing ourselves for the change of orientation and disposition that this implies is becoming our most urgent task.

In one of Plato's dialogues there is a character who says that man is like an upside-down tree, his roots planted aloft, far beyond the limits of the earth.[1] More than two thousand years later, and perhaps in a distant

1   Plato, *Timaeus*, 90a.

echo of Plato's words, Rivarol wrote: "Every state […] is a mysterious ship whose anchors are in the heavens."[2] That the context happened to be a defense of the old regime and of the religious principle of its legitimation matters little, and the idea need not even be limited to the political domain in general. We can easily take it beyond these bounds and venture to say that the anchors of humanity itself are in the heavens. If we are to save our capsizing ship, it is there that we must look.

---

2   Rivarol, *Discours préliminaire de son Nouveau Dictionnaire de la langue française.*

Index